WHINY LITTLE BITCH

The Excuse-Filled Presidency of Barack Obama

Mike Cullen

Quite Right Books

2010

Quite Right Books, LLC, Publisher
PO Box 80012
Raleigh, NC 27623

Printed in the United States of America

Cover design: Kreative Bomb (www.kreativebomb.com)

ISBN: 978-0-9845447-0-7

To Mom and Dad, for all the usual reasons;

and to Jackie, who knows everything about me, and understands.

CONTENTS

Introduction

The first thing I noticed about Barack Obama was his ego. The guy had a messianic complex large enough to keep a team of psychiatrists occupied for years. From atop the mountain, he once spake:

> *Generations from now, we will be able to look back and tell our children that this was the moment when we began to provide care for the sick and good jobs to the jobless; this was the moment when the rise of the oceans began to slow and our planet began to heal.*

This sounds like Ten Commandments type stuff. At very least it sounded like the most important day our country had seen since the signing of the Declaration of Independence. You might wonder, what great day in our history was Barack Obama describing?

June 3, 2008. He had just won a couple of primaries and clinched the Democrat nomination. That's it. But in Obama's mind it was a historic day. If you were 45 years old and had already written two books about yourself, you would probably think so too.

All of the ego stuff was cute, but it didn't seem likely to amount to much. How could the American people elect a guy with less executive experience than their local dry cleaner? The only way Obama could possibly become president was for Republicans to basically forfeit the race. John McCain, a.k.a. the Bob Dole of 2008, was the Republican equivalent of the forfeit Obama needed.

The second thing I noticed about Obama was his whining. Even after he became president, he could not stop himself from bashing his predecessor. It was unseemly and embarrassing. I initially wrote it off as the presidential equivalent of opening night jitters; the nervous babbling of a neophyte who had found himself out of his depth.

After a few months it had become annoying. Bill Clinton had spent eight years letting terrorists, foreign and domestic, run rampant. George Bush never uttered a peep about it. He rolled up his sleeves and did his best to fix the situation.

Every president inherits problems. The American people don't want to hear the president complain about them. We want him to put on his big-boy pants and deal with them.

After a year, the whining had become ridiculous. During his disastrously unsuccessful pitch for Martha Coakley – the Democrat who actually failed to retain Ted Kennedy's U.S. Senate seat in Massachusetts – Obama told the crowd "we have had one year to make up for eight." It was a laughable follow-up to the bloated egotism of his campaign – a constant reminder that we had elected the first affirmative action president, and we shouldn't expect much.

I had never seen anything like it. Only 43 men have held the office of President of the United States. This guy gets into office, and even one year later, he still can't stop sniveling about the man who held the position before him. Can you picture Abraham Lincoln engaging in a year-long whine about James Buchanan? I inherited this slavery problem, you know. So don't get your hopes too high.

The combination of balloon-sized ego and childish whining created an irresistible target. Obama is like the villain in a teen comedy film; the contemptible prig who ends up getting covered in paint or dog spit in act three. The title of this book was not imagined. It was earned.

The first year of the Obama administration moved quickly. It was like sitting on a bullet train and watching the bad governance zip past. Each new offense would push the previous one from our minds before we could fully digest its consequences.

While researching this book, I had a chance to slow down and document the damage. I would frequently run across an item that I had encountered briefly during that first year, and then forgotten. Details like Obama's hapless gift to the British Prime Minister, or his characterization of doctors as amputation-mad butchers, were pushed aside by more important issues. It was fun to revisit them here.

Like most tyrant wannabes, Barack Obama is a small and petty man. It's okay to laugh at him.

Rule Number One:
Barack Obama is Not Stupid

Every time a new president takes office there's a period of adjustment. It's not a honeymoon. It's more of a feeling-out process. We come to grips with the actual person who has assumed the office, as opposed to the campaign persona we saw during election season.

I didn't vote for Barack Obama, and it took me the better part of a year to figure him out as president. I kept running into the same question, posed in different ways on various issues.

Is this guy an idiot?

When he ordered the closing of Guantanamo Bay, even though he had no clue what we were going to do with the inmates housed therein, I wondered, "Have we elected a fool?"

When he appointed a publicly avowed Communist as his Green Jobs Czar, I asked, "Is Barack Obama a moron?"

When his solution for an economy that was overspent and saddled with debt was to spend a lot more and balloon the debt to historic levels, I asked anyone within earshot, "Is the leader of the free world a drooling, gibbering, falling-down dense, hockey puck head?"

The questions were maddening. Until I decided upon this president's general intelligence level, I would not be able to understand any of his decisions. An examination of his background was in order.

He attended Columbia University. It's a good school, but he didn't leave much of a mark there.

He attended Harvard Law School and became president of the Harvard Law Review. He then passed the bar exam. It's hard, though not impossible, for a dummy to do those things.

He worked as a community organizer.

He worked as a professor for twelve years at the University of Chicago. No points there. University professorship is, at best, intelligence neutral.

Measuring intelligence, even when you use I.Q. tests, is not something that can be done with precision. I finally decided, perhaps arbitrarily, that Barack Obama was not stupid. While he was clearly no genius, he was a man possessed of an above-average intellect.

With that single realization I had managed to clarify virtually every move Obama made. The sky opened. The angelic choir sang. With the excuse of stupidity removed, transparency had arrived.

Unfortunately for Obama, stupidity can be a pretty effective shield. When you remove stupidity from the equation, his motives appear unpleasantly cynical.

Was he stupid about Guantanamo? No. He just didn't care where we put the inmates. He cared about pandering to his lunatic base.

Was it stupid carelessness that led him to appoint Van Jones as the Green Jobs Czar. No. He knew full well that Jones was a Communist, but he appointed him anyway.

What about the economy? Obama's stimulus plan had no prayer of creating jobs, and he was smart enough to know it. But an $800 million plan that makes no sense as economic stimulus can make perfect sense as a vote-buying scheme.

An ideal example of Rule Number One came in Obama's 2009 Town Hall Meeting in Elkhart, Indiana. In defense of his tax credit plan he said:

> When you give a tax break to working families who are struggling, they will spend it on buying a new coat for the kids, or making sure that they get that car repaired that they use to get to work. When you give it to the wealthier families, they just put it away somewhere, and so it doesn't circulate in the economy.

"They just put it away somewhere." That's right, folks. If you sneak into Bill Gates' house you can find a big stack of Benjamins that he just "put away." It won't be in his mattress. Bill Gates is smarter than that. But it'll be there – put away – somewhere.

Barack Obama is a multi-millionaire. He knows what rich people do with money. They start businesses. They invest in companies that employ millions. They buy bonds that build schools and finance local governments. They do not hide it under that suspiciously-loose floorboard in the kitchen. Barack Obama knows this. He is not stupid enough to think otherwise. But in financially strapped Elkhart, it was a lie he thought he could sell.

At various times in the book I will refer to Rule Number One, and it is this: "Barack Obama is not stupid, but he hopes you might be."

Chapter One

With Friends Like Barack...

Barack Obama wanted the United States to reset its relationship with Russia. To prove his dedication to the concept, he dispatched his Secretary of State to drive the point home. Hillary Clinton arrived, wearing her best Jack Nicholson Joker smile, and presented the Russian Foreign Minister with "a little gift" – a gift-wrapped button with the word "reset" on it in Russian. The idea was that they would both press the symbolic button, thereby resetting the two countries' shared relationship. To which point in history would we be resetting? That wasn't made clear.

The event was a fitting summary of the Obama Administration's competence on foreign policy issues. The Russian Foreign Minister opened gift and discovered that the focused effort of the entire U.S. State Department was insufficient to discover the rare Russian word for "reset." Hillary's gift of a bright red reset button was actually emblazoned with the Russian word for "overcharge." Apparently she had given the Foreign Minister the button Obama had intended for the U.S. taxpayers.

They pressed the thing anyway.

A few months later, Obama scrapped plans for a missile defense shield in the Czech Republic and Poland, leaving those two nations wondering if the reset button was bringing us back to 1946. In exchange for betraying two NATO allies, we received – well, nothing. Obama deserves extra points for breaking the news on September 17, 2009 – the seventieth anniversary of the Soviet invasion of Poland.

Under the exciting new Obama regime, treating your allies with respect is part of the "failed policies of the past." Just ask Great Britain.

The bust of Winston Churchill – the great British leader, and only the second man ever to receive honorary U.S. citizenship – had been on loan to the U.S. from the British government. George W. Bush had displayed it with pride in the Oval Office. In spite of a British offer to extend the loan, Obama ordered the bust removed not just from the Oval Office, but from the White House entirely.

When British PM Gordon Brown arrived in Washington a few weeks later, Obama canceled the joint press conference that is traditional when an allied leader is in town. The given reason for the cancellation was "snow," which led the U.K Telegraph to wonder if at least a few of the 132 rooms in the White House were sufficiently snow-free to manage a press conference. No such luck.

If you think those little press conferences are silly – well, you're right. But they are also useful for the foreign leader in question. When you stand up there in front of your flag, and the president stands next to you, in front of the American flag, it's an invaluable photo op. It shows the people back home (and any tyrant around the world who is weighing the plusses and minuses of becoming a pain in your ass) that you're in tight with the United States of America. Since there was no pressing US/UK business to discuss, the photo op was pretty much the only reason for Brown to cross the Atlantic. Canceled. Lotta snow, you see.

During the traditional gift-giving portion of the visit, Brown presented Obama with an ornamental pen holder crafted from the timbers of the Victorian era anti-slave ship HMS Gannet. The Gannet was the sister ship to the HMS Resolute, the ship from which was crafted the famous "Resolute Desk," which has been in the White House since 1880. He also gave Obama the framed commission for the Resolute, and a seven-volume biography of Winston Churchill, signed by the author.

How did Barack Obama represent the United States in the traditional exchange of gifts? By presenting the Prime Minister of the United Kingdom with a box of 25 DVDs.

These weren't just any DVDs – they were once owned by Henry VIII. Okay, that last part I made up. They were just DVDs.

When Brown brought the DVDs back to England, a large crowd gathered. The English people were astonished by the shiny, spinning discs that made movies happen. Okay, I made that up too. They have DVDs in the U.K.

Since the days of World War II, the U.S. and the U.K. have shared what has been known as a "Special Relationship." The two countries have shared military bases, developed nuclear weapons together, shared intelligence, invested in each other's economy, and cooperated on countless matters large and small. When other nations failed to support us in Iraq, the U.K. was there. They are far and away the most reliable and trustworthy ally the United States has ever had.

The only people in America who didn't grasp this fact happened to work in Barack Obama's State Department. When asked by the British press why the Gordon Brown visit had been so low-key (a euphemism for "crappy and insulting"), a member of our State Department replied angrily, "There's nothing special about Britain. You're just the same as the other 190 countries in the world. You shouldn't expect special treatment."

A few weeks after the debacle at the White House, Obama had a chance to redeem himself during a meeting with Queen Elizabeth II. He gifted the queen with an iPod, though anyone with the ability to do a Google search would know the queen had owned one for years. This iPod was special, though. ~~It once belonged to Henry VIII.~~ Among other things, this iPod contained the speeches of that noted historical figure Barack Obama. In Obama's mind there is no greater gift than the sound of his voice.

It was a whirlwind year of international bone-headedness.

Obama's first state dinner was held in honor of Manmohan Singh, the Prime Minister of India. A pair of TV reality show wannabes evaded White House security and crashed the party. In a move certain to inspire confidence around the world, the unscreened crashers even shook hands with the Prime Minister himself. In spite of losing the game of Tag the Prime Minister, Singh, who had won a previous immunity challenge, was allowed to remain on the island.

Obama swept into Copenhagen to support Chicago's bid for the 2016 Olympic Games. Chicago was considered the frontrunner, and an appearance by the rock star President was supposed to seal the deal. After devoting five whole hours of his time to the multi-year bid, he flew out of town before the results were announced. The Olympic Committee found that Chicago's strengths – corruption, pollution and crime – were not enough to carry the day. The winning city of Rio de Janeiro was quite capable of matching Chicago on all three points, and had the added bonus of hot chicks on beaches.

World leaders from the Far East to the Middle East got a chance to check out Obama's bald spot, as he decided that a firm handshake is no longer a sufficient form of greeting. The President of the world's only superpower (check back for updates on that one) prefers to abase himself and his country by bowing to kings, emperors – and in one odd case – the mayor of Tampa, Florida.

The Canadian press thought Prime Minister Stephen Harper had been snubbed when he was met at the White House door by a minor protocol droid instead of the president. A quick call to the Canadian ambassador smoothed the whole thing over. Once the White House explained that it was Obama's policy to treat all of our allies like garbage, the Canadians were satisfied. They just didn't want to be singled out.

After famously vowing to meet with Iran "without preconditions," Obama found out Iran had their own set of conditions. No talks occurred, but Iran continued to build its nuclear program.

Speaking of a nuclear Iran, and speaking further of treating our allies like garbage, let's talk about Israel. You might remember them. Our only reliable ally in the Middle East? Is that ringing any bells? Here's one – their citizens are the ones not trying to blow up, decapitate or set our citizens on fire. Yeah. Them. Israel.

Obama the Candidate played the role of a strong supporter of Israel, at least when he was talking to Jews. In a speech to the American Israel Public Affairs Council, he reeeeally wanted them to believe he was pro-Israel. He even tossed them a "Let me be clear."

Let me be clear... Jerusalem will remain the capital of Israel, and it must remain undivided.

You might read that and think Obama felt an undivided Jerusalem should remain the capital of Israel. Hah! Shows how much you know. It took him almost no time at all to backtrack on CNN:

You know, the truth is that this was an example where we had some poor phrasing in the speech. And we immediately tried to correct the interpretation that was given.

What does that mean? On the matter of a divided Jerusalem, whose side was he on? Your guess is as good as Israel's.

Once he became president, Obama's first phone call to a foreign leader was to Mahmoud Abbas, Chairman of the PLO. There are plenty of actual world leaders he could have called – you know, men and women who run countries. Instead he chose to hook up with the Palestinians, that lovable cast of vagrants and terrorists. At that point, Israel pretty much knew it was going to be a rough four years.

Obama himself would not deign to visit our Middle East ally, but he did dispatch the administration's professional clown, Joe Biden.

Biden's job during his trip to Israel was simple –
he was there to take offense.

The intolerable act that launched a thousand
recriminations was this: Israel announced that
they had approved plans to build 1,600 housing
units in East Jerusalem. How dare they build
houses in the capital of Israel?!

What followed was an elaborate pantomime of
shock and offense. Pantomime Biden was furious,
and displayed his anger by showing up 90
minutes late for a meal with Israel's PM
Netanyahu. By the time he showed up, all the
best appetizers were gone. Pantomime Hillary
Clinton phoned Netanyahu a few days later to
voice her displeasure, to which Netanyahu
responded, "Oh, that's right. You're the Secretary
of State. Obama usually sends somebody else to
discuss the important stuff."

The big fun was reserved for a few weeks later
when Netanyahu visited the White House. Obama
wanted Netanyahu to halt construction in Israel's
capital city. That would make it much easier to
hand a chunk of the city over to the Palestinians
in a future deal. For some reason Netanyahu
wasn't really keen on the idea.

Faced with a genuine disagreement with an important ally, what did Obama do? Did he?

a.) Use his transcendent powers of persuasion and unification to smooth relations with the Israeli PM, sending Netanyahu home with a renewed respect for America.

b.) Stomp out of a meeting, leaving an invited guest adrift, while he went to dinner with Michelle and the kids.

If you guessed "a", you're living in the past. In Obama's America, we kick our friends in the teeth while we appease our enemies. The full extent of Obama's diplomacy was an over-the-shoulder wave as he headed off to dinner. "I'm still around," he said. "Let me know if there is anything new."

An Israeli paper said Netanyahu had received "the treatment reserved for the President of Equatorial Guinea," but I would disagree. Equatorial Guinea would have to be vital to U.S. interests, or at least become a reliable friend, before they deserved that kind of snub.

Chapter Two

Less Than Stimulating

This plan will save or create over three million jobs – almost all of them in the private sector.

- Barack Obama

You could write a comedy sketch about the early days of the Obama administration. You've got some amusing characters: the nose-in-the-air President, alternately pretending he's too cool for the job and then sniveling about all the bad things he "inherited"; the mentally unbalanced Speaker of the House, swooping in on her broom and waving her gavel; and the lovable goof of a Vice President, insulting foreign leaders, and occasionally piddling on the floor... But your sketch wouldn't work. The subject matter is too unbelievable.

The American Recovery and Reinvestment Act of 2009, better known as Obama's stimulus plan, exceeded anyone's most ridiculous exaggerations of tax-and-spend liberalism. It featured "tax cuts" that didn't alter the tax tables, almost $800 billion (yes, billion with a "b") in spending, and a Russian roulette method of paying for it that has not been explained to this day. It gave us the concept of a "saved job," the abuse of which we will no doubt experience for many administrations to come.

It was going to happen fast. Obama and his administration kept hammering the urgency of the matter. The economy was in bad shape. People were suffering. Something had to be done immediately. As in, right now. Joe Biden seemed to suggest the entire country had a bladder problem. "Quite simply, we cannot wait," he said. According to the Obama administration, we could not wait for the 3-4 million jobs the bill would create by the end of 2010. With unemployment rising, we could not delay this wonderful plan that would keep the unemployment rate below 8%. We had to spend a huge chunk of money immediately.

Republicans were skeptical. This single spending bill was larger than the annual GDP of all but 16 countries in the world. More than Switzerland. More than Sweden. More than Saudi Arabia. More than Austria. We're not talking about Burundi here. These are real countries. The Republicans looked at Obama and saw a man who had never held an executive position – never a mayor, never a governor, never a business owner, never ran so much as a lemonade stand – and wondered if he was the ideal mastermind for this particular bright idea. Before they trusted the entire GDP of Turkey to this guy and his plan, perhaps they should talk about it. Perhaps they should, you know, read the bill.

"Read the bill" became the rallying cry for Republicans who felt that such a large amount of money should be spent carefully. That was not about to happen. After months of closed-door tinkering, the bill was brought to the House late one night and debate began the next morning. At one point minority leader John Boehner dropped the 1,100 page bill on the floor of the House, and announced to the membership, "Not one of you has read this." If he was expecting to shame the Democrats, he was talking to the wrong people.

Democrat rep John Conyers summed up his party's stand on bill-reading: "I love these members, they get up and say, 'Read the bill!' What good is reading the bill if it's a thousand pages and you don't have two days and two lawyers to find out what it means after you read the bill?"

That's quite an admission by Conyers. Even though he is an elected member of the United States Congress, he doesn't see the point in reading lengthy bills. Even if he read them, he would be incapable of understanding them. You need only hear him speak for a minute to suspect the man of being a raging incompetent, but it's refreshing to see him announce it publicly.

The stimulus plan was rushed through the House and Senate with record speed, because the situation was too urgent to wait. We didn't have time to read the bill, because Americans were suffering, and they needed help immediately. Congress passed the bill on February 13. ~~Obama signed it the next day.~~ Obama signed it on February 17, after finally returning from a long Valentine's Day weekend in Chicago.

Once we got past the formality of creating a budget-destroying new law, we finally got a chance to see what was inside that big stack of paper. The final tab was $787 billion, which comes to slightly over $715 million per page. It featured $275 billion in tax credits, which Obama and Co. repeatedly referred to as tax cuts, either because they're lying, or because they truly do not understand the difference.

Tax credits

There's a few billion dollars for an expansion of the $1000 per child tax credit. To qualify for the payout you have to earn at least $3000 during the entire year. At minimum wage, that works out to eight bone-grinding hours a week, so try to pace yourself. If you manage to qualify, you can trade your kids for government cash. Wait, I might be reading that wrong. You get to keep the kids and the cash. And since we aren't living in Haiti, you'll probably manage to earn more than $3000.

They also expanded the earned income tax credit, which tosses another $4.7 billion into the mix. This one is for low income families with at least three children. If you qualify, pat yourself on the back and keep breeding. Between this tax credit and the one above, it's no wonder kids cost so much on the black market. They're walking, talking cash machines.

Then there's the part that most of us are familiar with – the $400 per person or $800 per couple tax credit. They couldn't cut you a check for this one. They had to dribble it to you at the rate of approximately $8 per week, presumably so you and the American economy wouldn't become overstimulated. That grimace on your boss's face comes from recalculating your federal withholding. He did it once in January, and then got to do it all over again in March. Now he's wondering how much money he could save if he laid your annoying ass off.

The tax credit was also responsible for its share of misery. Thousands of taxpayers received an unwelcome surprise when they filled out their 2009 taxes. Thanks to the new tax tables, many two-income families did not have enough tax withheld from their paychecks. The government gave them a tax credit twice as large as it should have been; leaving these couples with unexpected tax bills when they were expecting refunds. Can we let you keep more of your own money and still put you in debt? Yes we can!

But if you're a Democrat, the fun doesn't start until you begin spending. There's over $500 billion of spending in this act, and if you don't like it, Barack Obama will laugh at you. This is Obama from the transcript from his 02/05/2009 speech to the House Democratic Caucus Issues Conference (Nancy Pelosi, Steny Hoyer, James Clyburn and similar creatures). I left the "stage directions" in.

> *So then you get the argument, well, this is not a stimulus bill, this is a spending bill. What do you think a stimulus is? (Laughter and applause.) That's the whole point. No, seriously. (Laughter.) That's the point. (Applause.)*

Yuk yuk, chuckle chuckle. This is how liberal Dems act when they're among friends. They're absolutely certain that confiscating billions from taxpayers and pouring it into pet projects is the only possible way to stimulate an economy. If you disagree, then you're a target of laughter. If you point out that Ronald Reagan's tax cuts lifted the country out of a recession and created 35 million jobs, they'll accuse you of living in the past.

Who wants some free money?

Let's kick off the giveaway with $47 billion in new unemployment benefits, both in terms of longer benefits and more money per week. Because nothing says "healthy economy" like giving cash to people who don't work. If you want to stimulate the economy, it makes sense to examine the ways workers are incentivized. A tax cut incentivizes a worker to work harder, be more productive, earn more, and thus keep more of his money. Regular and larger unemployment checks incentivize the worker to beat that really hard level on God of War III.

There are billions of dollars in cash payments to the elderly, billions for construction, billions to subsidize health insurance, billions to subsidize Medicaid, billions to prevent layoffs in schools, billions to increase Pell grants, billions for special education, billions for low-income public schoolchildren, billions for more food stamps, billions for "temporary" welfare, billions for Head Start, and billions for the establishment for the Office of Federal High-Performance Green Buildings. Obama's stimulus plan reads like a liberal's Christmas list (or whichever non-sectarian, wicca-inspired gift-giving occasion they might choose). It's a cash bonanza for the Democrat base. When you have $500 billion to throw around, everyone gets paid.

It's difficult to see how printing more food stamps can boost a slow economy, but there are Democrats who will look you straight in the eye and make that claim. Rather than arguing these items individually, it makes more sense to judge the results. How did the stimulus do? Did it work?

Two-term Senator Evan Bayh didn't think so. Bayh is a Democrat. He had an inside view of this monstrosity as it was being built. After announcing his intention to leave the Senate and return to the private sector, Bayh said, "If I could create one job in the private sector by helping to grow a business, that's one more than Congress has created in the last six months." That puts the preliminary job count, particularly in the private sector, at zero.

If you're a fan of jobs then you're not a fan of this stimulus. The pledge to keep the unemployment rate below 8% was shattered instantly. Did the influx of cash keep the rate below 8.5%? No. 9%? Not quite. When the unemployment rate hit 9.5%, Joe Biden admitted, "We misread how bad the economy was," which wasn't so much an admission of failure as it was yet another shot at the previous administration. About Obama's stimulus Biden said, "This is just starting. The pace of the ball is now going to increase." I don't know what ball he was talking about, but if he had said, "The number of you becoming unemployed is now going to increase," he would have been exactly right. The unemployment rate jumped to 10.2%. When you take into account the workers who gave up the job search, the effective unemployment rate rose to 19.2%.

Not surprisingly, the Obama gang looked for other ways to describe the success of their plan. In July 2009 they began to shy away from the word "stimulus" and begin using "stabilization." Their story had changed. They weren't really trying to stimulate the economy; they wanted to stabilize it – to stop it from falling into a full-scale depression. While it does set the bar a lot lower, it also usurps the justification of another gigantic spending program – the $700 billion TARP program of 2008. TARP was sold to us as an emergency bailout that would stop the banks from failing, and thus save us from an economic collapse of biblical proportions. TARP was stabilization, and Obama has many times bragged that it worked. To believe the new spin, you had to believe that Obama's master plan was to follow stabilization with... more stabilization.

The most entertaining attempt to paint the stimulus as a success was the invention of the concept of the "saved job." Sure, we didn't create any jobs, but it would have been a whole lot worse if we weren't around. We saved a bunch of jobs. You see that group of guys working over there? We saved some of their jobs. We're not saying which ones, but... some of 'em.

One hundred days after the stimulus was signed, Obama claimed that it had already "saved or created 150,000 jobs." The boast gave pause to people who lived in the world of facts. It was a difficult claim to refute, because it was utterly fabricated. Disproving it was like disproving the existence of leprechauns. What was the definition of a saved job? If you saved my job on Monday, and I'm still working a month later, have you saved it again? To Obama, the definition was less important than the large number of "saved or created" jobs he would periodically report to the press.

Let The Fraud Begin!

Once you start playing the Saved Job Game, all things are possible.

An Indian tribe reported one job created thanks to their stimulus grant. What was the total dollar value of the grant? $1000. One whole job for a thousand bucks. Must have been the same guy who sold Manhattan to the Dutch for $24.

The town of Fairfield, CT received a grant for $37,000, with which they claimed to create an amazing 20 jobs. It was a huge breakthrough. At the cost of only $1850 per job the stimulus could create enough jobs to employ every man, woman and child in the United States... and Mexico. Sadly, this job bonanza was not to be. The money actually went to purchase laptops and patrol rifles.

Head Start programs across the country used the money to give cost-of-living raises to their employees. They then listed fictitious numbers of jobs saved or created. When pressed, they claimed they were only following the instructions given to them by the White House. The state of Nevada also received interesting White House instructions. They were told to take their total amount of stimulus cash and divide it by $92,000, and report that as their number of jobs created. At least 4000 bogus jobs were "created" by the trick.

In Washington, 24,000 phony teaching jobs were listed as saved. In fact, the teachers were already under contract. Their jobs were safe. In a financial shell game, the money that was going to pay them was shuffled to offset expenses elsewhere in the state budget, while they were paid by the stimulus cash.

In Texas, 5100 jobs were created for people age 24 and under. They turned out to be part-time summer jobs that lasted an average of 8 weeks. How many of the participants went on to full-time positions? "Maybe 25," said the placement company.

The state of California claimed that the stimulus cash saved 26,156 jobs in the California State University system, which would end up being over half of their employees. When pressed, the University system admitted they weren't about to lay off half of their workforce. A CSU spokeswoman said, "This is not really a real number of people. It's like a budget number." And you are not really a real spokeswoman.

The Obama administration dragged people into the deception. A Missouri school superintendent made the mistake of filling out his stimulus report form accurately. All of his hirings had been planned before the cash arrived, and there had been no plans for layoffs, therefore the number of jobs saved or created was zero. This earned him a scolding from a government official who explained that zero was an entirely unacceptable answer. The superintendent complied by plugging in some numbers that made the government happier.

Even if you buy Obama's saved job numbers (and if you do, please visit the AA branch in your city or town), it makes no sense to equate a saved job with a created job. Some jobs should not be saved. That's why we no longer have very many switchboard operators or typewriter manufacturers. A healthy economy creates new jobs based upon demand and eliminates the obsolete. Assuming there were saved jobs, how many of them should have been sloughed off like so much dead skin? It's hard to say. Okay. It's really, really, really hard to say. We still don't know what a saved job is.

One thing is certain; the United States economy is the strongest in the world. It will recover, possibly even during this administration. When that happens, every newspaper and television station whose name doesn't end in "ox" will tell you the same thing – the stimulus worked!

Chapter Three

A Lie Wrapped in a Whine

Joseph Goebbels is credited with saying, "If you repeat a lie often enough, it becomes the truth." Barack Obama chose to build his first year in office, and who knows how many more, on the following lie:

> *I inherited the $1.3 trillion deficit when I came into office.*

The Goebbels plan didn't come with an instruction book. He never stated how many repetitions were required. Obama decided to take no chances. He used various versions of the statement over 50 times in his first year's speeches, interviews and town hall meetings. Not a month went by without him restating it in some public place. He couldn't have invested more heavily in this lie if it was being sold by Bernie Madoff himself. It went a long way toward the formation of my picture of the man.

In my mind's eye I see Obama in an elegant restaurant. A tuxedoed waiter stands patiently nearby. After lengthy deliberation, Obama glances up at the waiter and says, "I inherited a $1.3 trillion deficit, and I'll start with the escargots."

As he headed into his second year as president, his Goebbels strategy was still going strong. He effortlessly weaved it into anything from fundraising speeches to the State of the Union itself. He had successfully sold the American people a lie. A charitable person might call it a half-truth, but that would be putting a pretty heavy discount on truth.

When Barack Obama entered the White House in 2009, he did not inherit a $1.3 trillion deficit. He inherited a projection. Fiscal 2009 was not over. In fact, it had only recently begun.

The 2009 fiscal year began in October 2008. The $1.3 trillion figure was a projection. A guess. An estimate of how bad things were going to get <u>if he didn't do anything to improve the economy</u>.

When Obama arrived, fiscal 2009 had eight months remaining. He had eight months to fight against the projection. He had eight months to institute some sort of (dare I say) change, designed to increase our revenues or decrease our spending. He did nothing of the sort. Obama embraced the dire projection. He saw it as a godsend. It was a license for him and his Democrat friends in Congress to spend billions.

On 02/05/09, he told the House Democrat Caucus:

I found this national debt, doubled, wrapped in a big bow waiting for me as I stepped into the Oval Office.

Obama's inheritance was a direct result of the spending spree that preceded his election – and every dime of that spending was a result of the "yea" vote of then-Senator Obama. When he stepped into the Oval Office, the only thing waiting for him was the luggage from his own voting record.

At some point cynicism takes over. The president lied. Well, lots of politicians lie. This particular politician lies so frequently and so effortlessly it can be hard to get worked up over one specific prevarication. But Obama's deficit lie served a second purpose. It was also an excuse.

The timing of his excuse making was stunning. He had just taken office. His administration was a few hours old. He had not yet attempted to do the job for which he was elected, but he was already disseminating excuses for his eventual failure. The narrative was simple: "My failure to fix the economy – and my fellow Americans, I promise you, I will fail. My failure is the fault of George W. Bush."

It's one thing to fail and then offer an excuse for your failure. Some excuses are valid, though we never like to hear them. It's an entirely different matter to offer excuses before you have even tried to do your job – tossing out bits of chaff to divert attention from your fecklessness.

That is the tactic of a whiny child.

> *Number one, we inherited a $1.3 trillion deficit – that wasn't from my – that wasn't me. That wasn't me.*

This was from a town hall meeting. I couldn't find a video of the event, so I'm not sure whether or not Obama was stamping his feet and pouting as he repeated, "That wasn't me. That wasn't me."

We've come a long way from the little wooden sign on Harry Truman's desk that told us plainly and unequivocally where the buck stopped. With this president, responsibility is a hot potato that must be passed as quickly as possible.

Whatever you do, you mustn't have the audacity to question or criticize our child-president. From a speech in New Orleans, this is how your questions appear to Obama:

> *You know, I listen to – sometimes – these reporters on the news, "Well, why haven't you solved world hunger yet? Why – it's been nine months."*

We don't need you to solve world hunger. We need you to grow up.

Chapter Four

Look who's coming to Washington – Janet Napolitano

Just hours after being confirmed as Barack Obama's Secretary of Homeland Security, Janet Napolitano got down to the business of making us all safer. She set her sights on that nagging problem of securing our border.

Our Northern border.

In one of her earliest directives as a cabinet member, Napolitano called attention to the insidious problem of Canadians crossing our border and threatening our very way of life. She said:

> *The Northern border of the United States has become, since 9/11, important to our national security. As we have designed programs to afford greater protection against unlawful entry, members of Congress and homeland security experts have called for increased attention to the Canadian border.*

You might have hoped that there was one single nook or cranny of this administration that wasn't infested by dangerous political correctness – and that it was Homeland Security. Unfortunately, hoping doesn't make it true. In the name of fairness, Napolitano wants us to treat Mexican and Canadian borders equally.

That's right. In Napolitano Math, twelve million unskilled intruders plus a few thousand murderous drug lords equals the occasional herd of rogue moose. We should treat both situations the same way.

If you think being equated with Mexico isn't insulting enough to our friends to the North, then get this. When addressing the press about her "Blame Canada" policy, she began rambling about the various terrorists who have entered the U.S., and claimed that the 9/11 terrorists entered the country through Canada.

Canada was not amused by the statement. While they might export excellent beers, they most certainly do not export suicide bombers, nor do they act as a way station for the latter.

Napolitano claimed her statement was based upon misunderstanding the question. Of course, she said, I know that the 9/11 terrorists didn't arrive via Canada. Okay. Yeah. It's easy to say it after the fact.

What else could she say? Admitting that you don't know jack about the 9/11 attacks is de facto evidence that you are not qualified to lead Homeland Security. But it does make you wonder about that earlier directive. The Canadian border has been an issue for how long?

Since 9/11.

It seems like a strange directive from someone who knows the 9/11 terrorists came from overseas. It makes sense coming from someone who thinks Canada is an exporter of terrorists.

While we remained on high alert at our Northern border, waiting for those murderous Canadians to make their move, things were a lot softer down South. Mexicans who entered our country illegally were thrilled to find out Napolitano's opinion of their actions. She told CNN that crossing our border illegally "is not a crime per se."

It is a crime "per law." That's strike two, Janet. Liberals might not see it as a crime, because they see illegal aliens as potential votes to be purchased with government handouts, but the word "illegal" in "illegal alien" still means what we think it means.

I was thinking about who I would want in charge of Homeland Security, and the guy who popped into my head was Colonel Flagg from M.A.S.H.. I want someone who is tough, humorless, and just a bit paranoid. I want someone who is looking for threats in places other people wouldn't think to check. That's what I want.

What I got was a Secretary of Homeland Security who is afraid to use the word "terrorism." She unveiled this gem in the early days of the administration. When enemies come into our country and proceed to destroy our buildings and murder our citizens, Napolitano calls this a "man-caused disaster." Now Janet, shouldn't that be "person-caused disaster?"

According to Napolitano, there is no need to differentiate between a multi-car accident on the interstate and a hijacked plane being smashed into a public building. They're both man-caused disasters.

She doesn't believe in terrorism, but she does believe in terrorists. A 2009 report released by Homeland Security tells us exactly where she plans to find them.

According to Napolitano, terrorists can be found on the political right. People who are displeased by our "Historic Presidential Election" could only be racists and should be viewed as potential terrorists. If you oppose illegal immigration you're one tiny step short of being a full-fledged terrorist. If you believe the second amendment gives you the right to bear arms, you need to be watched closely. You might crash a plane into a building tomorrow.

If you're a military veteran returning from the fight against Al-Qaeda or the Taliban, you'll be disappointed to find out that Homeland Security considers you as large a threat as the enemy you've been fighting. Says the report:

> *The possible passage of new restrictions on firearms and the return of military veterans facing significant challenges reintegrating into their communities could lead to the potential emergence of terrorist groups or lone wolf extremists capable of carrying out violent attacks.*

While the report admits it has "no specific information that domestic rightwing terrorists are currently planning acts of violence," Napolitano's Homeland Security department is going to keep one eye on you right-wingers. The other eye will remain trained on those wily Canadians.

Janet Napolitano is proof that there is at least one person in Washington who is less qualified for her job than Barack Obama is for his. When an actual terrorist took a shot at blowing up a planed bound for the U.S., we got a look at the kind of quality leadership she provides.

On Christmas Day of 2009, a young Nigerian named Umar Farouk Abdulmutallab tried to blow up a Northwest Airlines flight headed to Detroit from Amsterdam. He managed to waltz past security and bring liquid explosives onto a 278 passenger plane. After his first attempt to detonate only caused smoldering flames, a Dutch filmmaker jumped on him and prevented further attempts. As far as Napolitano was concerned, this was a pretty good result. "One thing I'd like to point out," she said, "is that the system worked."

Thanks, Janet. Is it my job to beat the crap out of the next terrorist you let on a plane, or can I trust that members of the Dutch film industry will be present on every flight?

Here's what happens when the system works. A young Nigerian kid comes down with a bad case of Islam. The kid's father, a respected banker in Nigeria, goes to the U.S. Embassy and tells them his kid has "become radicalized." He tells them that little Umar has gone to Yemen to participate in "some kind of jihad." Under our smoothly working system, Umar is then allowed to board a plane to the United States and set fire to his genitals.

Umar paid for his ticket in cash. He checked no luggage. He traveled alone. He might as well have been wearing an "I'm an Islamic Terrorist" t-shirt. None of it earned him an ounce of extra attention.

The system worked, you see.

Welcome to Washington, you person-caused disaster.

Chapter Five

And if you disagree with me...
You're a racist

I will listen to you,
especially when we disagree.

-Barack Obama, Election Night, 2008

It was a night for the simpleminded to frolic. Their messiah had been elected, and his words were beautiful. "I will listen to you, especially when we disagree," he said, and people cheered.

It's was a wonderful sentiment. It brought to mind our country's best tradition of free speech and robust debate. It was especially appealing to those who were under the impression that they had elected a uniter to our highest office. The quote was featured on a hundred liberal blogs before the sun rose the next morning. Many cited it as their favorite moment of the entire speech. They loved it. They believed it.

Like most of Obama's promises, this one didn't work out as advertised; and like most of his more distasteful personal attributes, his intolerance for dissent was obvious before we made the four-year mistake. His stated love of bipartisanship was only campaign-deep. His record told a different story.

During his brief experience in the Senate, he was its most partisan member, topping the 2007 National Journal list of most liberal senators. Based upon his voting record, Obama was more liberal than Jim DeMint was conservative. Cross the aisle? He couldn't even see the aisle from where he was sitting.

As we entered the homestretch of the 2008 campaign, Obama abruptly decided to add some additional Chicago media to his campaign jet. Rather than squeezing a few extra reporters into the mix, some members of the press would be dropped. The unlucky victims represented the New York Post, The Washington Times, and the Dallas Morning News.

What did these three organizations have in common? They were all daily newspapers in large cities. Their reporters had diligently covered the campaign since its early days. Unfortunately for the reporters involved, in a country where virtually every major newspaper issues a rubber-stamp endorsement of the Democrat candidate, all three of their papers had endorsed John McCain for president. A Washington Times reporter had traveled with Obama for three solid years, and 72 hours after his paper endorsed McCain, their guy got the boot.

The representative from Glamour magazine remained on the plane, so we were not robbed of the type of hard-hitting journalism only Glamour can provide.

After his soaring election night pledge, the stimulus bill gave Obama his first chance to back up the promise. When Republicans were called in to discuss the plan, Obama dismissed their ideas out of hand. What was the reason for his sudden closed-mindedness? "I won," he explained.

At a campaign rally later in the year, in one of his trademark whines, he blamed the poor economy on the Republicans for perhaps the thousandth time. Then he added a new twist. He said:

> But I don't want the folks who created the mess to do a lot of talking. I want them to get out of the way so we can clean up the mess. I don't mind cleaning up after them, but don't do a lot of talking.

It paints a pretty clear picture of how he views dissent. I will listen to you, especially when we disagree. But it would be better for everyone if you didn't do a lot of talking.

Autumn brought us the White House's war against Fox News, launched by Obama's claim that, "I've got one television station that is entirely devoted to attacking my administration." The next time Obama made the rounds of the Sunday political shows, Fox News' request for an interview was denied. White House communications director Anita Dunn called Fox News, "a wing of the Republican Party," and confirmed that the refusal was intentional and a direct response to Fox News's non-conforming viewpoint.

The reaction showcased Obama's enormous sense of entitlement. In a television news world where NBC, ABC, CBS, CNBC, CNN, and MSNBC acted as Obama's cheerleaders during the campaign, and as his loyal servants ever since, his reaction went beyond childish. There was exactly one television news network willing to criticize him, but the existence of that single network was enough to send the president into a foot-stamping tantrum. Even The Nation, normally a reliably left-wing publication, found Obama's tantrum unseemly, causing them to brand him the "Whiner-in-Chief."

You can have your blind partisanship and press intimidation. For my money, nothing crushes dissent like a good old-fashioned enemies list. And what better place to compile it than at whitehouse.gov? In August 2009 Obama devoted a section of the official White House website to collecting information about those who disagreed with his health care plan. Supporter-collaborators were instructed to report "fishy" statements about health insurance reform to flag@whitehouse.gov. There's no mention of how loyal comrades would be rewarded, but I'm guessing there might be an extra ration of fresh fruit for somebody special.

It has been a recurring pattern in the Obama presidency – grand calls for bipartisanship mixed with chilling, sometimes Orwellian, reactions to dissent.

The outcome of a February 2010 heath reform meeting with Republicans was predictable to everyone except the president. Obama, like a broken robot that keeps rebooting and running the same stale programming, seemed to assume that legislators with opposing viewpoints would capitulate once they were bathed in the light of his brilliance. When Republicans had the temerity to disagree with his plan, Obama became snippy and petulant. His one-liners lost their humor, but the bitterness remained. He interrupted speakers at his leisure. He informed Senator McCain that, "we're not campaigning anymore. The election is over." When Congressman Eric Cantor had the audacity to arrive with a hard copy printout of the bill under discussion, Obama called it a "prop." By the end of the discussion, Obama had spent more time speaking than all 17 Republicans combined. I will listen to you, but you'll hardly get a word in, since I am The President Who Never Shuts Up.

When all else fails, Obama can fall back upon the ultimate safety net – his blackness. Since we were introduced to Obama the candidate, there has been a constant drumbeat directed against dissenters. Vocal critics are branded as racists, and an unknown number of potential critics are deterred by their fear of such an accusation. His Race Brigade is large and it starts at home.

A few days after the election, wife Michelle introduced us to "Barack, The Race Victim" in a 60 Minutes interview. "The realities are, as a black man, Barack can get shot going to the gas station," she said.

It is our silent shame to live in a country where so many black men are gunned down trying to top off with ethanol.

Jimmy Carter, the current holder of the title America's Most Embarrassing President, showed great sportsmanship in supporting Obama's attempt to claim the crown. Carter showed his support with a textbook example of painting dissent as racism. "I think an overwhelming portion of the intensely demonstrated animosity toward President Barack Obama is based on the fact that he is a black man, that he's African-American," he said.

Carter later realized that his race-baiting should have been a little more subtle. He had helped Obama at the cost of his own credibility. Jimmy backpedaled from the original statement, and claimed he was misquoted. He must have forgotten that we now have those newfangled doohickeys that record all the words you say. I mean, they're a hoot. You talk into them, and they play back words that sound just like you.

Then there were the Tea Parties. While you can find liberals protesting everything from animal rights to trans fats, it's historically difficult to get conservatives to assemble in large numbers. You see, conservatives have jobs. Some of them have children they actually choose to raise. It's tough to get them to rallies, because they have other things to do. The government's fiscal irresponsibility gave birth to the Tea Party movement, a group of people who were so fed up with the Obama spend-a-thon, they were willing to put the rest of their lives on hold to speak out against it.

The Tea Party movement quickly became a significant political force, figuring prominently in the losses of Democrat governors in Virginia and New Jersey, and the hilarious loss of Ted Kennedy's Senate seat in Massachusetts. Obama's minions chose the first and most reliable play from their playbook – attempting to brand the dissenters as racists.

When the Tea Partiers failed to show themselves as actual racists, extreme measures were required. Numerous liberal websites were launched simultaneously, almost as if they had been following instructions from higher-up. These sites urged their readers to infiltrate the Tea Parties and discredit them by committing various bad acts, including yelling racial epithets and carrying racist signs. Since bathing and combing your hair were requirements for posing as a Tea Partier, a sufficient number of infiltrators could not be found.

C-List Hollywood teamed up with D-List television when Janeane Garofalo got together with Keith Olbermann to discuss the 2009 tax day Tea Party rallies. Don't remember Janeane? When they needed a grotesquely ugly girl to star opposite Uma Thurman, they fished Janeane out of a nearby swamp. She had the very innovative idea that people who disagree with our shiny, new president are racists. "This is about hating a black man in the White House," she said. "This is racism straight up."

With all due respect to malodorous Hollywood-types, no one carries Obama's water as dutifully as the press. After Congressman Joe Wilson accurately informed the president "You lie!" during a live, televised speech, something had to be done. Maureen Dowd responded in the New York Times with a piece that went three steps past bizarre.

According to Maureen, when Joe Wilson spoke, there was "an unspoken word in the air." What Maureen heard was, "You lie, boy!"

Huh?

What?

It was an unspoken word. For those of us who have been raised to see and treat others equally, it was also an unthought-of word. It takes an especially twisted psyche to invent such a connection.

At some point you have to wonder about Freudian projection. What goes through Maureen Dowd's mind when she sees someone with dark skin? Is every black man a hair's breadth from taking up residence on Maureen's mental plantation?

While the rest of society has moved past this odd "race first" method of viewing others, liberal commentators can't help themselves. Pinning the "racist" tag on political opponents is fun. It's a club they can't stop swinging.

MSNBC's Chris Matthews let his obsession with race get the best of him after Obama's first State of the Union speech. In his usual long-winded gush, he declared that Obama's oration was so excellent, "I forgot he was black tonight for an hour."

I picture Matthews at night, waiting for sleep to come. While the rest of us count sheep, you can hear him mumbling, "My president is black. My president is black. My president is black."

Congratulations, Chris. One whole hour. That's excellent progress for you. You're now just 8,759 hours away from living the normal life the rest of us live.

If Joe Wilson can be accused of racism for things he never said, it's a short leap in logic to redefine existing words after people say them. Critics of Obama, we are told, tend to use "code words" to camouflage their racially-based hatred.

Barack Obama served as a professor at the University of Chicago Law School, but if you call him a professor, you're a racist. Harvard law professor Charles Ogletree sees the word "professor" as a thinly-veiled attack on Obama's race. "Calling Obama the professor walks dangerously close to labeling him uppity," says Ogletree. Hmm. I had always thought people who called Obama "professorial" were using it as a euphemism for "cold." I thought they were being nice, but I guess they were actually being racists.

In just over a year, Obama's government took control of banks, car companies, the entire student loan program, and the health care industry. If you describe this behavior as socialist, you're a racist. MSNBC talking head Carlos Watson fears that "socialist is becoming a code word," and that "socialist is becoming the new n-word."

The phrase "code word" is becoming a code word. It means "I couldn't find any racist language in what you said, but I desperately need people to think you are a racist. Please. It's all I've got."

I just looked back a few paragraphs, and was shocked to find that I had used the word "night." I should probably remove it. It begins with the letters "n-i-g."

After long deliberation, I decided to leave the offending word in place. The left would only find something else to complain about.

Chapter Six

He Lies!

You lie!

- Joe Wilson (R), South Carolina

We were all raised to tell the truth, but Congressman Joe Wilson learned that there's a certain place and time where the truth is not welcome.

The place is Washington, DC. The time is any time Barack Obama is speaking.

During the address to the Joint Session of Congress, Obama had just finished saying:

> *There are also those who claim that our reform effort will insure illegal immigrants. This, too, is false. The reforms I'm proposing would not apply to those who are here illegally.*

In truth, the plan essentially said that it would not insure illegals, but it would never check to see if they were illegals. The obvious end result would be all-you-can-eat health coverage for anyone who claimed to be in the country legally, even if they had to do it through an interpreter. Wilson had recently backed two amendments that would have closed the loophole, but both had been shot down in flames by the Democrats.

In a speech filled with half-truths and outright whoppers, this particular Obama prevarication barely registered with most listeners, but thanks to his recent legislative struggles, it hit Wilson like a thunderbolt.

"You lie!" he yelled.

Chaos ensued. Grumbles and boos echoed throughout the chamber. Nancy Pelosi's most recent facelift came completely undone. Never before had stating the obvious brought so much attention to one man.

Wilson had not only called the president a liar, but he had committed a transgression against the rules of the occasion, where groaning and making faces is acceptable, but actual bits of discernable language are verboten. Wilson had sinned against protocol and dissed decorum.

There is a culture inside Washington that values, above all other things, the culture inside Washington. Protocol and decorum will win the tag-team battle against health care and national defense every time. If everybody plays nice, then we'll all get to divvy up three trillion dollars in taxpayer money each year. Four trillion when the Democrats are in charge.

Politicians from both parties were quick to pound the protruding nail.

South Carolina rep Jim Clyburn said Wilson's objection "went beyond heckling. That was probably one of the most insulting things I've ever seen."

If that's the kind of reprimand the two words "You lie" gets you, then Joe Wilson didn't get his money's worth. He could have told Obama what he really thought of him, and the backlash wouldn't have been much worse. And it would have made Clyburn's statement look less ridiculous.

John McCain, who never met a Republican he couldn't slam in the press, but goes strangely mute when pitted against Democrats, said the outburst was "totally disrespectful. There is no place for it in that setting, or any other, and he should apologize for it immediately."

According to McCain, you can't call the President on a lie in that setting *or any other*. So if the President were to churn out an absurd whopper like, "John McCain ran an excellent campaign in 2008," there is actually no appropriate setting in which to challenge it.

Beyond placing Band-Aids on the various cuts and scrapes endured by protocol, there wasn't much discussion of the point of Wilson's objection – the President of the United States, while discussing an important issue in front of the full membership of Congress and a live national audience – was making stuff up. Some people care about such things, but they tend not to reside in Washington.

When Wilson said, "You lie," he was presumably addressing a single statement on health care reform, but he could easily have meant it to apply generally to almost any public statement Obama makes.

Chapter Seven

Now You C it, Now You Don't

We will work on this process publicly. It will be on C-Span. It will be streaming over the net.

- Barack Obama

A man with Barack Obama's beliefs is bound to be divisive. He has a far-left voting record and a list of Marxist friends and influences that is many pages long. In the 2008 election, liberals were bound to support him, and conservatives were guaranteed to oppose him. The reaction to his plan to bring the United States health care system under state control was mixed, with both camps choosing the obvious position.

Only one of Obama's promises appealed to members of both sides – his pledge that the negotiations that made up the health care debate would be telecast on C-Span, "so the public will be part of the conversation." The pledge was a big deal. He mentioned it numerous times during the campaign, and it was a huge applause line every time he used it.

It should have been. Most legislative negotiations occur behind closed doors. Politicians disappear, sometimes for hours at a time, before finally emerging from their sequestration and lying to us. The opportunity to see what actually goes on in those backrooms, especially on such an important issue, had wide appeal.

"I can't guarantee it'll be exciting," said Obama, during his seventh recitation of the promise. It turns out he couldn't guarantee anything.

Obama promised change. When you look at his 2008 campaign, and you look beyond the stadium shows and the pyrotechnics, beyond the race-baiting he employed, beyond the supporters who could faint on cue (and always seemed to be sitting in the front row), the C-Span promise was the only thing that sounded like actual change. It was the one single genuine thing that even his detractors had to admit would be a change from the status-quo.

It was a lie.

It was change we couldn't, or at least shouldn't have believed in.

The negotiations behind health care reform were the sleaziest kind of Washington-business-as-usual politics. Deals were cut and payoffs were made in exact same way such negotiations have always been held – behind closed doors.

Obama courted and received the endorsements of the American Nurses Association and the AARP, over the objections of thousands of their members.

Hospitals were next, agreeing to give up $155 billion in payments over ten years, because we all know hospitals have too much damn money. The hospital deal sounded like a plea bargain offered to a perp. You agree to this much abuse now, and we'll call the whole thing off. If you let this case go to a trial (or to Congress), you might end up with the death penalty.

Most amusing was the deal Obama and his administration cut with the pharmaceutical companies. The Huffington Post, presumably irate because the deal did not involve the slow execution of the people who manufacture our medicine, published what they purported to be a memo outlining the points of the agreement. Obama dispatched a spokesman who denounced the memo as false, but felt no obligation to tell anyone which parts were false. He was quick to brag about the $80 billion in savings he had negotiated from big PhRMA, but was completely closemouthed about what he had given up in return.

All anyone could do was speculate about the details of these deals, because none of the talks were televised. None of the congressional discussions were on C-Span either, though it would have been nice to have them televised – if only for sake of the Republicans – who weren't invited to participate in person.

As Democrat majorities in both houses crafted their bills, the public, even without the benefit of C-Span, began to discover the contents of the legislation. Obama's response was to tell Congress to hurry up. He wanted a finished bill by the August recess. It didn't happen. What followed were the Town Halls of 2009.

Members of Congress frequently schedule town hall meetings in their district during the August recess. The Pol stands on a stage while members of a sparse audience, comprised mostly of people who worked on his last campaign, compete to see who can lob him the highest arching softball. That is, until 2009.

During the Town Halls of 2009 actual concerned citizens showed up, armed with pointed questions for their representatives. Most of the questions concerned the proposed health care takeover. House Speaker Nancy Pelosi referred to these citizens as Nazis, thereby fulfilling the president's pledge that the public would be "part of the discussion."

The town halls ended. On November 7th the House passed their version of the bill. It is posted on their website. The first document is titled "A Robust and Transparent Health Reform Debate." Got to give them credit for big brass ones.

The Senate was a bit more oily. They gathered on Christmas Eve, in the early morning. Anyone in America who was not still in bed was out trying to find his kid a Zhu Zhu Pet. They staged a quick vote, passed their bill, and flew home. It was the first time the Senate had voted on Christmas Eve since 1895.

Two health care bills, negotiated in secret, had been passed. Not only had Obama failed to get the negotiations televised, he had never asked Congress to do so. Not once. He gave Congress a pass, and the press gave him a pass.

We never even got to the point where he got to claim it wasn't his fault. I can almost hear him lecturing, "In this country we have something called separation of powers. That means I can't just call up the Congress and tell them what to do." He gets to keep that excuse in his pocket.

C-Span was still game. Even at this late stage, they were scrambling for even a tiny shred of the president's promised transparency. In a letter to the various involved parties, C-Span CEO Brian Lamb wrote:

> *President Obama, Senate and House leaders, many of your rank-and-file members, and the nation's editorial pages have all talked about the value of transparent discussions on reforming the nation's health care system. Now that the process moves to the critical stage of reconciliation between the Chambers, we*

respectfully request that you allow the public full access, through television, to legislation that will affect the lives of every single American.

So far, no change.

Chapter Eight

Look Who's Coming to Washington – ACORN

Back in 1970, the organization known as ACORN (The Association of Community Organizations for Reform Now) was founded. Back then, it was all about fighting "the Man" and keeping the welfare checks moving.

Fast forward to 2010 and you'll see ACORN is still around, now all grown up as a full-fledged criminal organization. When you see the words "community organizer" on Barack Obama's resume, ACORN is the job description.

ACORN experienced the usual growing pains – a small matter of embezzlement, involving the founder and his brother. But who really cares about a stray million bucks here or there when donors and governments are footing the bills?

ACORN is constantly pushing for a higher minimum wage, as long as it doesn't apply to them. They even sued the state of California, claiming that they should be excluded from the state's minimum wage law. What was their reasoning? In a legal brief they claimed, "The more that ACORN must pay each individual outreach worker—either because of minimum or overtime requirements—the fewer outreach workers it will be able to hire." The state decided that while outreach workers might be unskilled dullards, they are entitled to the same minimum wage as burger flippers and amusement park ride operators.

ACORN is ostensibly pro-union, but that doesn't extend to their own workers. In 2003, the National Labor Relations Board ordered ACORN to rehire and pay restitution to employees who were fired when attempting to organize a union. The employees were trying to improve upon ACORN's notoriously low pay and 54-hour work week.

ACORN employees in multiple locations were famously caught on camera in 2009 offering help to two activists who were posing as a pimp and prostitute. Start-up businesses can be tough, and the pimp and prostitute needed help. They were planning to start a brothel using imported girls from El Salvador. How could they start their prostitution ring in a financially responsible way?

The very cooperative folks at ACORN were a wellspring of helpful suggestions. They had money management tips for the prostitute, which included claiming she was a "freelancer" or a "performance artist" on any financial forms. They also offered her advice on laundering her cash.

There was good news for the pimp. Since the El Salvadoran girls he planned to import were underage, the folks at ACORN had advice on how he could claim them as dependents. He could also use his prostitute girlfriend's earnings as a down payment for a "no doc" home loan, which would allow him to purchase the whorehouse of his dreams! Sure, it's a fixer-upper. But the underage El Salvadorans girls are an almost endless supply of free labor.

In case you were wondering if this was just some sort of misunderstanding, there's this bit of sage advice from an ACORN office administrator in Brooklyn: "Don't get caught. It's against the law what you are doing, and there's a chance you'll get caught."

ACORN's reaction to the tapes was not so much a response as it was epileptic spasm. Within a few days, ACORN execs informed us that:

1) The charges were not true.
2) The employees in question had been fired.
3) The tapes had been doctored.
4) The employees did not represent the high standards of ACORN.
5) They were going to sue the people who made the tapes, FOX News, and anyone else who dared to show them.
6) The employees on the tapes were not really ACORN employees at all, but were only seasonal help, because presumably, you need to hire extra help during the busy brothel-establishment season.

While facilitating prostitution and tax fraud might be an entertaining way to spend an afternoon, they shouldn't deflect attention from ACORN's primary mission – election fraud. This is what they do best, and this is why Barack Obama loves them.

ACORN likes to register new voters. Why is this necessary, you might ask? Registering to vote is monumentally simple. You can do it by printing out an internet form. A one-minute search revealed over 30 places where I could register, and that's just in my county. None of that is good enough for ACORN. They don't want me. If you're too stupid – or lazy – or apathetic to get yourself registered, then answer that knock on your door. ACORN is looking for you.

Using cash from primarily Democrat sources, they hire unskilled workers to troll their way through low income neighborhoods in an attempt to produce scrapings from the bottom of the electoral barrel. The workers are often forced to meet daily registration quotas or risk termination. If you think this sort of quota is illegal in most states, you're right. If you think ACORN cares, you're wrong. At least 17 states have pursued election fraud cases against ACORN.

Most of the newly-registered are poor and/or minorities, but ACORN isn't especially picky. Membership in the human race is not even a requirement.

In Florida, thanks to ACORN, Mickey Mouse registered to vote. Mickey lives in Orlando (natch), and has never been convicted of a felony.

ACORN registered O'jahnae Smith, age 7, to vote in Connecticut.

In 2008, an ACORN group in Nevada submitted the Dallas Cowboys starting lineup as new registrants, but they couldn't fool Secretary of State Ross Miller. "Tony Romo is not registered to vote in the state of Nevada, and anybody trying to pose as Terrell Owens won't be able to cast a ballot on Nov. 4."

As our Community-Organizer-in-Chief, what kind of relationship does Barack Obama have with this Association of Community Organizers? That depends on who you are, and when you ask him the question. In a CNN interview, during the heart of the 2008 Presidential campaign, he said this:

> *My relationship with ACORN is pretty straightforward. It's probably thirteen years ago, when I was still practicing law. I represented ACORN, and my partner in that representation was the U.S. Justice Department, in having Illionis implement what was called the Motor Voter Law. To make sure that people could go to DMVs and driver's license facilities to get registered. It wasn't being implemented. That was my relationship and is my relationship to ACORN.*

That doesn't sound so bad. After all, he was working alongside the Justice Department, and nothing bad ever happens there. You might come to wonder how young lawyer Obama came to represent ACORN. Did they pick his name out of a phone book?

In a taped meeting with ACORN officials, the then-Senator Obama told them this:

> *I definitely welcome ACORN's input. You don't have to ask me about that. I'm gonna call you, even if you didn't ask me.*

> *When I ran Project Vote, the voter registration drive in Illinois, ACORN was smack dab in the middle of it.*

> *Once I was elected, there wasn't a campaign that ACORN worked on, down in Springfield, that I wasn't right there with you.*

> *Since I've been in the United States Senate, I've been always a partner with ACORN as well.*

> *I've been fighting with ACORN, alongside ACORN, on the issues you care about, my entire career.*

With Obama, the truth is always flexible. There's one version for the CNN audience and another for the ACORN activists. He needs one group to like him and the other to work for him.

In retrospect, the CNN audience got robbed, because there was some nice cash attached to working for Obama. His campaign doled out over $800,000 to an ACORN subsidiary, most of it for "staging, sound and lighting." If you think "staging, sound and lighting" seems like an unusual thing to purchase from ACORN, you're not alone. The Federal Election Commission thought so too. After being questioned about the expense, Obama amended his FEC documents. The purpose of the payment was "get out the vote" efforts. Right in ACORN's fraudulent wheelhouse.

While $800,000 sounds like a lot of money, you can't argue with ACORN's results. After all, that vote from Donald Duck could have been the one that put Obama over the top.

Addendum: In early 2010, ACORN announced it would be "dissolved as a national structure." This is the fallout from the 2009 pimp and prostitute sting.

After an initial moment of amusement, I realized that this was not exactly a thrilling result. There was some advantage in having Obama's sleazy accomplices out in the open and operating under a widely-identifiable name. Now each local organization will have to be identified and combated individually.

Chapter Nine

The President Acted Stupidly

In July 2009, law enforcement received a report of a possible break-in at a Cambridge, MA home. The police, led by Sgt. James Crowley, arrived at the residence to investigate the report.

As Sgt. Crowley arrived at the home, he had reason to believe a crime might be in progress. According to the police report, he saw Henry Louis Gates, a 58-year-old black man, through the front door glass. He asked Gates to step outside, and Gates replied, "No I will not."

Sgt. Crowley identified himself and said he was investigating a report of a break-in in progress. Gates opened the door and asked, "why, because I'm a black man in America?"

Gates had recently arrived home and found his front door stuck shut. With the help of his driver, Gates had forced the door open. A witness had reported the incident to 911 as a forced entry into a home, because that's what it was. The situation has a certain sitcom feel to it: Tonight on Malcolm in the Middle, Hal is arrested for breaking into his own house. A more rational man might find humor in the situation, and understand that it can be easily resolved by producing identification. Gates instead responded with a bizarre and immediate hostility.

At this point in the encounter, Sgt. Crowley did not know if a crime had been committed, nor did he know if he was speaking to the rightful resident of the home. Logic dictated that he attempt to confirm these facts. Through Gates' screamed accusations of racism, Sgt. Crowley requested, and after an initial refusal, received a Harvard University identification card from Gates. Sgt. Crowley radioed the Harvard University Police and requested their presence.

Gates continued to scream. Sgt. Crowley left the home in an effort to find a quieter place to use his radio. Gates followed, and from his rant we can discern these things:

1)   Sgt. Crowley was a racist cop.
2)   Sgt. Crowley didn't know who he was "messing" with.
3)   Sgt. Crowley had not heard the last of this.

When Sgt. Crowley arrived outside, he discovered a crowd of onlookers was forming. Gates followed him outside and continued his loud and abusive behavior. Sgt. Crowley informed him that he was becoming disorderly. Gates continued his outburst, drawing the attention of more onlookers. Sgt. Crowley warned him again, and took out his handcuffs.

I didn't grow up in one of the rougher neighborhoods in America, but even I know what it means when a cop takes out his handcuffs. Apparently Gates did not. He continued his screaming, and got himself arrested for disorderly conduct.

The arrest blew up into a national incident, with charges of racism and racial profiling hurled against Sgt. Crowley. How dare he arrest a black man in his own house! Something must be done.

Into this firestorm wandered Barack Obama, the man who was supposed to usher America into a new post-racial age. While it really wasn't the type of situation into which the president should poke his nose, perhaps he could take a few minutes away from his efforts to lower the sea levels and smooth out this little tiff.

At a press conference purportedly for the discussion of health care legislation, Obama was asked a question about the Gates blowup. After manipulating the question order to make sure that it was the last one in the press conference, he received it with no apparent surprise. What did our bridger-of-racial-divides tell us?

Well, I should say at the outset that "Skip" Gates is a friend, so I may be a little biased here. I don't know all the facts.

For a president who is looking for an opportunity to act presidential, there were a few good openings here. He could have gone with the "Skip

Gates is my friend" angle, therefore it is inappropriate for me to comment. He could have chosen the "I don't know all the facts" angle, therefore it is unwise of me to comment. Even without those two convenient tools, there's always the "I'm the damned president, and it doesn't help anyone if I shoot off my damned mouth about some damned police matter in Massachusetts" angle, which would have worked every bit as well. Here's what we got:

> *Now, I don't know, not having been there and not seeing all the facts...*

Roughly translated: I don't have the facts, but allow me to comment at length...

It's like watching CNN cover a breaking news story. They don't know what's going on. They have no facts, but they've got a helicopter shot of a bunch of people standing around, and they think there might be a dog stuck in a drainage ditch. Whatever it is, they're going to sit there in the studio and keep talking, because the only alternative is to switch you back to Anderson Cooper 360. And nobody wants that.

> *I think it's fair to say, number one, any of us would be pretty angry; number two, that the Cambridge Police acted stupidly in arresting somebody when there was already proof that they were in their own home.*

Hmm. I wasn't there, but the police acted stupidly. That line would be one of the dumbest things Joe Biden ever said. This brings us back to Rule Number One. It's Obama giving us the "is he stupid or not" choice. I have chosen to believe that Barack Obama is not stupid, so I assume the statement is intentional. The statement is also designed to focus anger against a white policeman for his actions against a black perpetrator. That too is intentional.

I also like the phrasing, "any of us would be pretty angry." Who is "us?" He was at a press conference. Maybe he meant, "us members of the press," but I don't think so. As far as anger is concerned, let's remember that Gates wasn't angry because he was arrested; he was arrested because he was angry. His anger began the moment he saw a policeman, a white policeman in particular, on his doorstep. It's quite common for "us" to blame our troubles on white policemen.

Having bashed the Cambridge Police in particular, it was now time to impugn police officers everywhere.

> *and number three, what I think we know separate and apart from this incident is that there is a long history in this country of African Americans and Latinos being stopped by law enforcement disproportionately. That's just a fact.*

> *When I was in the state legislature in Illinois, we worked on a racial profiling bill because there was indisputable evidence that blacks and Hispanics were being stopped*

disproportionately. And that is a sign, an example of how, you know, race remains a factor in this society. That doesn't lessen the incredible progress that has been made. I am standing here as testimony to the progress that's been made.

And yet the fact of the matter is, is that this still haunts us. And even when there are honest misunderstandings, the fact that blacks and Hispanics are picked up more frequently and oftentime for no cause casts suspicion even when there is good cause. And that's why I think the more that we're working with local law enforcement to improve policing techniques so that we're eliminating potential bias, the safer everybody is going to be.

It's a pretty lengthy statement from a guy who wasn't there, and admits he doesn't know the facts. It's also quite a diatribe for a situation where the proper – and presidential – comment is "no comment."

What should we have expected from Obama? Based upon the election year hype, he would have said something transcendent – something that would make everyone feel better about the situation. After seeing the man in office for a year, it's obviously an absurd expectation, but it's the type of thing millions of Obama voters thought they were getting.

Instead, he showed himself to be a racial partisan straight from the Al Sharpton mold.

Thanks for the healing, Barack.

Chapter Ten

Hating for Fun and (no) Profit

I did not run for office to be helping out a bunch of you know, fat cat bankers on Wall Street.

- Barack Obama

You weren't really expecting a uniter, were you? When we inaugurated a community organizer – a professional agitator – you didn't think it would bring us all together. Did you?

The sales pitch we received during the campaign was typified by Obama crony Cass Sunstein in the Huffington Post. In his gushing deification of Obama, Sunstein concluded that the future President Obama would be a "genuine uniter."

At the time it was a ridiculous thing to say about a man whose voting record made him the most liberal member of the United States Senate – a man with a Marxist/leftist background and an almost perfect unwillingness to work across the aisle. In retrospect, it is even sillier. After just over a year in office, Barack Obama had polarized the nation more severely than any other president in recent memory. One of the tools he used to achieve this, his desired result, was the manipulation of class envy.

The Ten Commandments order us not to covet the belongings of others, but as the commandments go, it is far from the most rigidly observed. For most of us, if we manage to avoid stealing, murdering or committing adultery, we've ticked off the most important boxes on the list. It is human nature to want things. We all desire to improve our lives. A little coveting never hurt anyone. The manipulation of that coveting, however, can be dangerous.

Adolph Hitler manipulated class envy effectively. During a time of economic depression and high unemployment, he sold the idea that the relatively well-to-do Jews were the cause of Germany's ills. In order to rally support for himself, he cast the Jews as objects of hatred.

Before your eyes glaze over at mention of Der Fuhrer, consider the case of AIG.

AIG was the American insurance company that collapsed during the financial meltdown in 2008, was judged "too big to fail," and was subsequently bailed out with taxpayer cash. As part of the deal, some AIG employees were to receive $165 million in contractually obligated bonuses. The bonuses were explicitly protected by the enormous, Democrat-written stimulus bill which was signed by Obama himself.

I'll repeat that last part, because it is important. The Democrats wrote the bill and Obama signed it.

Obama then turned around and labeled the bonuses an "outrage." He railed against the greed of AIG, spurring protests at many of the company's offices, and death threats to AIG employees and their families. Protesters from the Connecticut Working Families Party (Obama's preferred combination of union thugs, ACORN, and other "community organizations") demonstrated outside the homes of AIG employees.

Many AIG employees voluntarily returned the bonuses they had legally earned, in an effort to preserve their own safety.

Whenever Barack Obama wants something done, his instructions to his mob are simple. Go hate somebody.

He chooses his targets from the ranks of the successful. The target is almost always from the private sector. He makes speeches and gives interviews, or sends out attack dogs to do the same, vilifying the target. He tells us the target is the cause of our problems, and we are urged to hate them. Don't worry, though. Obama has a plan for this evil target, who has caused us all this pain. The solution sometimes involves dragging the target into a congressional hearing, where he gets to spend a day and a half trying to understand what Barney Frank is saying. The solution always involves taking the target's money.

Let's take a look at doctors. You know, the people who take care of you when you get sick. You might be positively inclined towards your doctor if you didn't have Barack Obama to set you straight. At a town hall meeting in Portsmouth, NH, this is how Obama described the way a diabetic patient gets treated:

> *If a family care physician works with his or her patient to help them lose weight, modify diet, monitors whether they're taking their medications in a timely fashion, they might get reimbursed a pittance. But if that same diabetic ends up getting their foot amputated, that's $30,000, $40,000, $50,000 -- immediately the surgeon is reimbursed.*

According to Obama, your doctor could save your health, but he would rather cut off your feet for some extra pocket cash.

First of all, a surgeon can not buy a new speedboat with the money he gets from lopping off your foot. The AMA reports that a surgeon makes around $700 for such a procedure. If you're thinking that was a tremendously stupid mistake for Obama to make, please refer back to Rule Number One.

Obama was trying to achieve something by saying such a thing. This was not an off-the-cuff comment. This was a prepared statement. He wants you to think your doctor is trying to rip you off and threaten your health. He wants you to be angry at your doctor. And by the way, he has a nice new health plan that will let you get even with that nasty doctor.

Think it was a fluke? Here's what he told the press in a news conference in July 2009. Ear, nose and throat docs beware... or maybe we should beware of you.

> *So if they're looking -- and you come in and you've got a bad sore throat, or your child has a bad sore throat or has repeated sore throats, the doctor may look at the reimbursement system and say to himself, you know what, I make a lot more money if I take this kid's tonsils out.*

In the class envy argument the motivation is always money, and the target is always portrayed as greedy. This is what Obama thinks of people in the private sector, and it's what he wants you to think of them too. It's a lot easier to support a plan for the government to control payments to doctors if you think your physician is performing unnecessary surgery on children.

Insurance companies are convenient targets. Dealing with them is difficult. They are steeped in regulations – government regulations, by the way. They are also profitable private sector businesses, which makes them a perfect target for the Obama hate campaign.

His stated goal is to put insurance companies out of business, and replace them with a single (government) payer system. In a speech to the AFL/CIO, he couldn't have been more plain:

> *I happen to be a proponent of a single-payer universal health care plan.*

He knows he can't do it himself, so he wants you to help him. The best way, or at least the only way he knows, is to get you to hate the insurance companies. Here's what he told a Pennsylvania crowd about insurance companies and their evil profits:

> *And they will keep on doing this for as long as they can get away with it. This is no secret. They're telling their investors this: We are in the money; we are going to keep on making big profits even though a lot of folks are going to be put under hardship.*

Obama loves to talk about the insurance industry earning "record profits." It isn't true, but it helps gin up the hate machine. Insurance company profits have been falling steadily for the last few years. Like most businesses, they have suffered during the slow economy.

The AMA national insurance report card shows that Medicare denies a larger percentage of claims than any insurance company in America. If the government is your health insurer, you are twice as likely to have your claim denied than you would have been with a private insurer. None of that registers with Obama, as he reels off sob story after sob story. He insists the insurance companies are horrible. They must be stopped. But don't worry, he's got a plan.

The Enemies List is long. Bankers are fat cats. Pharmaceutical companies are greedy. He even took on the Chamber of Commerce. They are all part and parcel of The Rich, the eternal enemy of Marxists and community organizers everywhere.

Demonizing the successful has worked well for Obama politically, but as he moves through the second year of his presidency, he has a problem. The country needs jobs, and he is unwilling to produce them. Yes. Unwilling. Read on.

New jobs come from entrepreneurs – people who start new businesses, hoping to create their own market or better serve an existing one. It's tough. It's risky. But for now at least, it can be very rewarding financially.

In rough numbers, here's what happens to 100 start-up businesses:

Eighty fail – That's a sizable majority. Some flame out spectacularly, while burning through piles of cash. Others putter along until their owner runs out of money or patience.

Sixteen are moderately successful – They employ a dozen people or fewer. They provide modest livings for their owners and maybe a few others.

Three are significantly successful – They employ up to 100 people. Their owners make very good money. Many employees have above average salaries and benefits.

One is a big success – This one rare business employs hundreds, or sometimes thousands of people. Revenues are huge. Jobs with benefits abound. The owner is rich.

There are four business owners on this list who get it. These four didn't get here by accident. The average successful business owner starts 3-5 businesses that fail before he learns the skills he needs to succeed. They know what it takes to start and build a business. Put simply, they are where jobs come from.

Once apprised of that little secret, the solution should be easy. Go to these people and ask them what they need to create more jobs.

The list would be long, but it would begin with money. Up to 39% of corporate income is taken from the people who know how to use it and handed over to numbskulls like Harry Reid and Nancy Pelosi. It's hard to create jobs when Congress keeps taking your money and spending it on Government Tattoo Removal for gang members. Give these entrepreneurs their money back, and get out of their way.

That's why it won't happen. These successful entrepreneurs are rich. Obama is too politically invested in making us hate them to suddenly turn around and let them keep more of their money.

Even if he knew they would use that money to grow the economy, the questions from his hate-base would be too difficult.

"Why are you giving those fat cats a tax cut?"

"Because they can produce millions of jobs and save the economy."

"That sounds like a very good thing, so why have you been telling us to hate them?"

You can see why we'll never walk down this road.

Chapter Eleven

Look Who's Coming to Washington – Van Jones

I met all these young radical people of color.
I mean really radical, communists
and anarchists. And it was, like,
'This is what I need to be a part of.'

- Van Jones

If you hate America, there's a good chance you can find yourself a place in the Obama administration. Socialists, Communists and Mao worshippers are welcome. Racists are encouraged to apply, as long as their hatred runs in the politically correct direction.

Van Jones fits the mold beautifully. He's an apologist for a cop-killer. He blames George W. Bush for Hurricane Katrina, and the bursting of the levees in New Orleans. He believes the United States brought the 9/11 attack on itself. He also signed the 9/11 truth statement from the nuts who believe Bush knew about 9/11 and deliberately allowed it to occur (he then un-signed it when the political heat got too heavy). He once bragged, "You've never seen a Columbine done by a black child."

He was a member of STORM (Standing Together to Organize a Revolutionary Movement), a group dedicated to uphold "revolutionary democracy, revolutionary feminism, revolutionary internationalism, the central role of the working class, urban Marxism, and Third World Communism."

Jones is a self-avowed Communist who, like many fellow travelers, found a comfortable home in the environmental movement. By espousing some odd plan that involved releasing imprisoned criminals and having them build solar panels, Van Jones the Marxist agitator became Van Jones the environmentally conscious. It was this new and improved Van Jones that Barack Obama chose as the Green Jobs Czar in March 2009. The official title was Special Advisor on Green Jobs, Enterprise and Innovation for the White House Council on Environmental Quality, but I won't make you read that again.

Don't think that Jones' magical transformation from militant thug to tree hugger was gradual, or that it was even a genuine change. Jones was kind enough to fill us in on his strategy. In a 2005 interview he explained, "I'm willing to forgo the cheap satisfaction of the radical pose for the deep satisfaction of radical ends."

Roughly translated for the folks back in Oakland: Don't worry, guys. I'm still the America hatin' dude you know and love. I'm just going to spend a couple of years pretending to be a Capitalist, and see where that gets me. I'm going to change my tactics and try to build our Marxist utopia from inside the government.

The problem is you're supposed to whisper those things, not announce them to the public. The truth about Jones was available to anyone willing to hear it.

The widespread revelation of Jones' past led to calls for him to step down or be fired. He resigned from the Green Jobs post in September 2009, among the traditional "none of it is true, but I don't want to be a distraction" baloney.

How could Obama appoint such a man to a federal government post? How could he have not known all these things about Jones?

When answering these questions, it is helpful to consult Rule Number One. Barack Obama is not stupid (but he thinks you might be). If your 90-year-old grandma can do a Google search and find Van Jones bragging about being a Communist, then so can the president. Which leads us to the only other available option – Obama knew exactly who Van Jones was, and Van Jones was exactly the kind of man Obama wanted to bring into our federal government.

Just because Jones is gone from the Green Jobs position, don't think he's gone for good. He didn't even leave Washington. He landed at the Center for American Progress, a left wing think tank funded by George Soros. This group recently announced that Americans and their use of cell phones are responsible for a war in the mineral-rich Democratic Republic of Congo. Jones should be right at home there.

In February 2010, Jones received an NAACP Image Award. NAACP head Benjamin Jealous called Jones an "American treasure."

Welcome to Washington, comrade.

Chapter Twelve

Closing the Islam Inn

So for example, I closed Guantanamo.
That was the right thing to do.

- Barack Obama, 03/19/2009

It's always interesting to examine what a president does in his first few days in office. It took Bill Clinton nine days to unveil his "Don't Ask, Don't Tell" policy for homosexuals in the U.S. military. In retrospect, it turned out to be a pretty accurate guide to Clintonian behavior. Go out and have sex with whomever you please, just don't tell anyone about it.

Two days into his presidency, Barack Obama showed us what was important to him. He signed an executive order calling for the closure of the Guantanamo Bay detention facility within one year. He wasn't much for plans or directions. He signed the order, and then it became one of those, "get back to me when it's done" projects he seems to enjoy (see healthcare).

Obama must have received some poor information, since in a 3/19/09 town hall meeting he talked about the closing of Gitmo as if it was a done deal. He spoke of it in the past tense. In a 4/3/09 town hall, he did it again:

In dealing with terrorism, we can't lose sight of our values and who we are. That's why I closed Guantanamo.

You've got to shake your head at the guy. He does love the word "I." The United States didn't close Gitmo. Barack Obama closed Gitmo.

Except, of course, he didn't. If you look inside the cells at Gitmo, the continued presence of murderous little men with scraggly beards should be your first clue. Obama did not close Guantanamo in March, nor did he close it in April. Come back at the end of the year. That's what he said in the executive order. Fair enough.

At the time of Obama's inauguration there were approximately 245 detainees at Gitmo. One year later the tally was 193. For the mathematically impaired, that means that Obama and his administration managed to deal with only 52 detainees in their first year in office. At that pace, a four-year presidential term won't be enough time to get the place closed.

Perhaps that's the plan. The pledge to close Guantanamo worked well as an election year issue. Maybe Obama is considering recycling the promise in 2012. He'd only have 37 detainees left. He could even promise to do it in one year.

In spite of Obama's soaring election year rhetoric, the people who voted for him (those who still admit it) have set the bar pretty low. To those people, knocking 52 noggins off the Gitmo headcount sounds like a reasonable year's work. Even if the pace is not what they had hoped for, at least he made a good start of undoing the evil of George W. Bush. Except that Bush was not particularly evil, especially when it came to releasing Guantanamo prisoners.

Since the war in Afghanistan began, the Guantanamo Bay detention facility has housed approximately 775 inmates. After the early years of the war, which consisted mostly of gathering and incarcerating enemy combatants, Gitmo detainees were being released at a rate of over 100 per year, or about twice the rate we witnessed under Obama the Liberator. By the end of the Bush administration, 530 inmates had been convicted or released. This isn't the sort of thing you hear very often, because it goes against the common perception of Guantanamo as a place where roaches check in, but they don't check out.

In November 2009, after it had become eminently clear that Obama's executive order was worth little more than kindling, he discussed the failure with Major Garrett of Fox News. When asked how disappointed he was about the missed deadline, Obama replied:

You know I'm not disappointed, I knew this was going to be hard, ah, it's hard not only because of the politics, people I think understandably are fearful after a lot of years where they were told that Guantanamo was critical to keeping terrorists out.

"Harder than you thought it would be?" asked Garrett.

No, as hard, I just think as usual in Washington things move slower than I anticipated.

His first quote translates as: "It's Bush's fault! He brainwashed people into thinking these terrorists were dangerous, now I can't get anyone to take them."

The second quote is borderline pathological. Even in the face of his colossal failure, he won't admit that the task was tougher than he thought it would be. He's basically saying, "Hey, you know that promise I made in January? I knew we had no shot at all of getting that one done."

As for things moving slower in Washington than he anticipated, feel free to choose your own villain. He could be blaming Congress, or Republicans, or the Beltway media, or even the DC Metro subway system. The one person he is not blaming is Barack Hussein Obama, who despite being a resident of the town for five years, has managed to avoid the mysterious slowing disease lurking therein.

It would be laughable to watch him dodge responsibility as shamelessly as a small child, save for the fact that this child is the President of the United States. After one year of his antics, it would be disingenuous to say I expected better. We most certainly deserve better.

Why is closing Guantanamo, to use the president's description, hard? Gitmo is populated by scum, with a hierarchy that ranges from mass murderers at the top, to wannabe mass murderers in the middle, to an oily base of extremist foot soldiers at the bottom. Closing the detention facility involves more than simply turning the deadbolt on the front door. You have to find an appropriate place to send each and every one of our jihadist friends, and nobody wants them. The same nations who criticize our terrible, unfair treatment of these heroic Muslims blanch at the prospect of taking even a small handful of them into their own prison systems.

So yes, it's hard. It's no harder now than when Obama signed his executive order. He insists it's exactly, precisely, the same amount of hard he expected. But it's too hard to do in one year, or even two.

That brings us to Thomson, Illinois. This small farming town has the twin misfortune of being home to a mostly empty prison, and having a Democrat governor in need of cash. For somewhere in excess of 100 million Obamabucks, Illinois Governor Pat Quinn has offered to sell the prison to the Feds for the expressed purpose of housing the Guantanamo misfits. The local folks have mixed feelings.

People who still have their sanity remind us that Thomson Ill. is a slightly softer target than the military-encrusted base on the Eastern edge of Cuba. Even when you remove the possibility of prisoner escapes, there's still a significant danger to the communities near the prison. Various people – visitors, let's say – can hop on a bus to Thomson. They can take a look around and discover all the possibilities of rural Illinois. Maybe some of them will travel a few dozen miles east and tour the nuclear plant.

Proponents of the plan point out that it will create 3000 jobs. That's all that many people care about. The Obama economy has slipped to such depths that having your neighborhood become a target for Muslim extremists is a small price to pay for one of those plum, high-quality prison guard jobs.

One of Governor Quinn's top aides tried to convince his fellow Illinoisans to take one for the team. Even though every Muslim with a pair of C4 underpants would be Google Mapping Western Illinois, the transfer would make the other 49 United States safer. "We all have the duty to sacrifice for each other," he said.

Fortunately, sacrificing the citizens of Illinois will have to wait for a while. Even though President

Obama has ordered the federal government to purchase the Thomson facility, it isn't a done deal. A purchase price has to be negotiated, and Congress has to part with the cash. Then the new facility will have to be upgraded, at a cost of millions of dollars, in order to provide the illusion of sufficient security. All of this must be completed before enough people have bouts of sanity that would scuttle the whole deal. The sunniest scenario should push the broken promise into 2011, at least.

But you remember what Obama said. It's hard.

Chapter Thirteen

Obama on Pork: Not Quite Kosher

Absolutely we need earmark reform. And when I'm president, I will go line by line to make sure that we are not spending money unwisely.

- Barack Obama

In February 2009, Barack Obama and his Democrat Congress spent $787 million in phantom cash on the American Recovery and Reinvestment Act of 2009. This steaming pile of law is what people are talking about when they refer to "the stimulus." The Reinvestment Act ended up being about as stimulating as a DVD full of Ralph Nader speeches, but it did provide an opportunity for Obama to show off his new, tough-on-earmarks presidency.

Earmarks, the longtime target of Obama's opponent John McCain, are those happy little bags of cash that lawmakers like to send back home to the constituents. Nothing says love like the new Fruit Fly Facility being constructed back in your home district. It's how a congressman says, "I'm looking out for you." It's also how he says, "You'd better vote for me if you want the gravy train to keep rolling."

In order to match McCain's fervor on the campaign trail, Obama promised earmark reform. Opinions on what constitutes an earmark can vary, but the number of earmarks in the stimulus were somewhere between zero and not many. It looked as if he was serious about keeping the promise.

Only four weeks later, he signed the Omnibus Appropriations Act of 2009. Historically, this is the annual spending bill with the worst earmark infestation. I was eager to see what Obama would do with it. It didn't take me long to find $800,000 for Oyster Rehabilitation in Alabama. As I continued to browse the excruciating bill, it didn't get worse. It stayed exactly the same. You might even say there was no change.

If the president was true to his word, and went over the bill line by line, here are some things he found. He must have thought they were great ideas, since he signed the bill without objection.

We've got $300,000 for a World Trade Center in Montana, $950,000 for a World Trade Center in St. Louis, and $385,000 for a World Trade Center in Utah. Apparently, the Obama administration has taken a new approach to terrorism. Rather than hunting and killing terrorists, we will now just build World Trade Centers faster than the terrorists can destroy them.

Democrat Dan Inouye dipped into the till, grabbing $250,000 in swag for the Polynesian Voyaging Society. Inouye sticks us with this tab annually. He claims it has "renewed interest in maritime exploration and reawakened native Hawaiian pride in environmental awareness and ocean stewardship." For those who don't speak Hawaiian, he's telling you to say "Aloha" to your money. Keep a close eye on that renewed interest in maritime exploration, though. If the underprivileged Polynesians manage to find a few more continents that we have not previously noticed, well, who'll be laughing then?

Inouye has a veritable fountain of worthy causes, all of them in Hawaii. He got $2 million "for the promotion of astronomy" in his state. Never mind that Hawaii is already considered one of the clearest places on Earth to view the stars, or that it already has hundreds of millions of dollars worth of astronomy facilities. They need your cash. If Inouye has to choose between braces for your daughter or a new telescope on Mauna Kea, your kid's overbite can wait.

There's $143,000 to the American Ballet Theater in New York, basically forcing kids K-12 to watch ballet. If we had pulled a stunt like that at Gitmo, Amnesty International would have gone crazy.

If you and your gang buddies have spent the last few years busting heads, dealing drugs, and generally terrorizing the citizens of Los Angeles, the government has a $200,000 cash prize for you. The people who brought you the Department of Motor Vehicles now bring you Government Tattoo Removal. Get it done now, before your next lineup!

Finally, there's a topic near and dear to us all – beaver management. Until 1939, North Carolina was beaver-free, but the rodents were reintroduced to the state's ecology in order to regain the kind of environmental benefits that only beavers can provide. Unfortunately, a few bad beavers can ruin things for everyone. When flooding from their dams threatens woodlands or railways, the beavers must be "managed." One manages a beaver by luring it into a trap, which kills it instantly, and then sending in a demolition team to destroy the beaver's dam with explosives, no doubt as an object lesson to other beavers. For that kind of quality entertainment, the $208,000 price tag seems about right.

I'll spare you the other 9280 examples. That's right, Barack "line-by-line" Obama signed off on a budgeting monstrosity with over 9000 earmarks, the second-worst total in the country's history. If you're looking for the number of pork projects he killed, I'll give you a hint: it's lower than the number of tax cheats in his cabinet.

The scheme was as cynical as it was transparent. No wonder the stimulus had been earmark-free. Lawmakers had been promised an all-you-can-eat pork buffet just a few weeks later. And everyone knows that you want to be good and hungry before hitting the buffet.

Obama was prepared to face the inevitable criticism. He had armed himself, as usual, with an excuse. Because parts of the bill had been negotiated in the previous year, before he had been elected, he dismissed the waste as "last year's business."

What? The job does come with a veto pen, particularly if you're vetoing "the failed policies of the past."

The childish go-to move of blaming Bush makes even less sense than usual in this case. The reason this crap was held over until 2009 is because even the free-spending George Bush wouldn't sign it. The Democrats held it over from 2008, and waited for Obama to take office. They were counting on him being a man of low character – hoping that his word meant nothing. He didn't disappoint them.

Along with the "last year's business" talking point, Obama, Chief of Staff Rahm Emanual and Spokesman Robert Gibbs all made vague promises for improvement in 2010.

At this writing, the 2010 Omnibus Spending Bill is at 10,000 earmarks and counting.

Chapter Fourteen

The 7 Habits of a Highly Ineffective President

How do you build an arrogant and unqualified excuse for a president? Start with these Barack Obama traits, and you'll be well on your way to creating your own laughing stock in a suit.

Habit #1: I Didn't Explain it Right

Barack Obama is never wrong. Just ask him. When one of his policies triggers the collective gag reflex of the American people, Obama says, "I didn't explain it right." There's nothing wrong with the policy. You yokels are too stupid to understand it.

After 11 months of speeches, town halls, press conferences, 60 Minutes interviews and weekly radio addresses, only 35% of the public supported his health care overhaul.

Let's put that 35% figure in its proper perspective. If Barack Obama went on a televised killing spree with a machete and a blow torch, about 35% of the American people would say he was framed –

or he must have had a good reason. About 35% of the public will support him in anything. Any. Thing.

So when 35% of the American people supported his health care plan; that means he managed to persuade nobody. No minds were changed. Eleven months of blowharditude accomplished nothing.

He then proceeded to stand up in the State of the Union address and tell us we should all love his health care plan, but he must not have explained it right.

Habit #2: Let Me Be Clear

This is Barack Obama's favorite phrase. After reading the transcripts of over 300 Obama speeches, I know all about "Let me be clear." It's the precursor to some of his most (ahem) audacious lies. It translates roughly as "Here comes a big one."

"Let me be clear" is the rhetorical equivalent of an exploding dye pack in a bag of cash. It indelibly marks all words that follow as false. Here's how he used it on the matter of General Motors.

> *Let me be clear: The United States government has no interest in running GM. We have no intention of running GM.*

Not long after this statement, Obama replaced the CEO of GM with his own flunky. Not long after that, the United States government owned 60% of General Motors.

Habit #3: Conflation

Conflation involves treating two distinct concepts as if they were one. It's an Obama favorite.

In an attempt to marginalize the Tea Party movement, Obama described them as people who question whether he is a U.S. citizen and believe he is a socialist.

Those are two different things. He is conflating them.

The people who question Obama's citizenship have plenty of questions, but not a lot of evidence. They are not an effective political force. Obama would love to stamp all of his critics with the "Birther" label, because he sees that as a battle that has already been won.

The people who consider Obama a socialist have a great deal of evidence. They have his communist mentor from Hawaii. They have his stated preference for Marxist professors. They have his numerous close associations with dangerous radicals like Jeremiah Wright, Van Jones, and Bill Ayers. Most of all, they have his policies: from taking over the largest car maker in America to taking over the American health care system.

If you are a Birther, you're on the fringe. If you think Barack Obama is a socialist, that only proves that you're paying attention. Don't let him conflate the two.

For extra credit, watch him discuss illegal aliens. If you oppose people entering our country illegally, you are "anti illegal immigration." This is a good thing. Your president will conflate your beliefs with something abhorrent, by branding you "anti immigration" or even "anti immigrant."

Habit #4: The False Choice

If someone offered you the choice of a punch in the nose or a kick in the groin, you might choose the punch in the nose, because you expect it to hurt less. More likely, you would ask if there was some third option that didn't involve excruciating pain on your part.

When Americans look to their government for responsible solutions, Barack Obama loves to offer us the false choice. We can either support his stale brand of socialism or we can do nothing.

"Inaction is not an option," he likes to say. If you don't like his stimulus plan or his energy plan he will tell you the same thing. Doing nothing is not an option. He will ignore the ideas of others while presenting his own plan as the only water in the desert.

It's either one or the other. Either we sign onto the latest product of Nancy Pelosi's diseased brain, or we do nothing. It's the classic false choice. Don't buy into it.

And what's so terrible about doing nothing? If Barack Obama can win the Nobel Peace Prize by doing nothing, then maybe inaction deserves a closer look.

Habit #5: The False Promise

When Obama said he would close Guantanamo Bay in a year, it was an ordinary lie. He could have done it, but he didn't.

The false promise is different than an ordinary lie. It requires an additional level of salesmanship. You have to convince your target that you have powers you do not possess.

When Obama claimed the health care negotiations would be broadcast on CSpan, it was a false promise. Obama doesn't control CSpan, and he certainly doesn't control the legislative branch. He could have pushed to make his promise come true. He could have tried. But he lacked the fundamental power to make good on his pledge.

Perhaps the most gullible victim of the false promise was Michigan Democrat Bart Stupak. The pro-life Stupak controlled a handful of key votes on Obama's health care bill. He was willing to support the legislation, but only if the new law prohibited federal funding of abortions.

Stupak didn't get his change. He lent his pivotal support in exchange for a Barack Obama false promise. Obama promised Stupak he would issue an executive order prohibiting federal funding of abortions, and he did so.

What's wrong with this deal? Presidents can't just change signed legislation to suit their needs. If they could, why would we need the legislative branch of government at all? The executive order was worthless. The abortion loophole was signed into law. Bart Stupak sold his vote for a bag of magic beans.

Habit #6: Blaming Your Opponents

Obama's whining about George Bush is well-documented. During the campaign it was acceptable. Once Obama took office it should have stopped. A year after Obama took office, it revealed him as an immature child.

Even more bizarre were his repeated attempts to blame Republicans for his own failures. With an overwhelming Democrat majority in the House, and a filibuster-proof majority in the Senate, he still didn't sign a single piece of major legislation in 2009.

He shifted the blame for his failures to Republicans, who he claimed were obstructionists and "the party of no."

Who would buy such an absurd notion? Once you rule out the people with functioning neurons, you're left with the 35% from Habit #1. Blaming the Republicans is always red meat for Obama's core constituency of social panhandlers, union thugs, and freelance left-wing bedwetter types.

Habit #7: Talking out of Your Ass

When our president speaks, we would like him to be thoughtful in his choice of words.

Maybe next time.

In situations that require a careful, measured (let's say "presidential") response, Barack Obama comes across like the barroom drunk who thinks he's an expert on everything. Facts are not important. Barry's got something to say, and it's a free country, dammit.

When his pal Skip Gates got himself arrested, Barry was right there to tell us that the police acted stupidly.

When Umar Abdulmutallab tried to blow up a plane full of people on Christmas Day, Barry put our minds at ease by describing him as an "isolated extremist." Umar was actually a gift from our Muslim friends at al Qaeda in Yemen, and it might have benefited our national security if we had treated him that way.

The city of Las Vegas has been a repeat victim of Obama's thoughtless rambling. In a 2009 town hall meeting, he warned executives from bailout companies to avoid the city or face his wrath. With the Vegas tourism business already suffering during the slow economy, city officials reported multiple cancellations in the days following Obama's remark. An insincere apology followed.

One year later he took another shot at Sin City, saying, "You don't blow a bunch of cash on Vegas when you're trying to save for college."

Las Vegas mayor Oscar Goodman provided a succinct summation of Obama's off-the-prompter behavior.

"This president is a real slow learner."

Chapter Fifteen

Domiciles for Deadbeats

*This economic crisis began as a financial crisis,
when banks and financial institutions took huge,
reckless risks in pursuit of quick profits and
massive bonuses.*

- Barack Obama

It began with bad intentions. Don't be fooled into
thinking otherwise. The housing collapse that set
off the financial crisis of 2007-2010 (and beyond)
was a rock that rolled downhill and squashed a
large number of people. The rock didn't slip. It
didn't shake loose over the normal course of time.
It was pushed.

To see how it all began, we need to go back past
the beginning. The Federal National Mortgage
Association (aka FNMA, aka Fannie Mae) was
founded in 1938 as a government enterprise, and
was converted to a private, stockholder-owned
corporation in 1968. The Federal Home Loan
Mortgage Corporation (aka FHLMC, aka Freddie
Mac) was created by the government in 1970 as a

private corporation designed to compete with Fannie Mae.

Fannie Mae and Freddie Mac purchase home mortgages from lenders, package the mortgages into securities, and sell them to investors on the open market. This provides mortgage lenders with the liquidity they need to continue making mortgage loans, and it provides investors with a good return on their investment, assuming the homeowners pay their mortgages.

The other piece of our puzzle is a 1977 law known as The Community Reinvestment Act. The CRA was designed to combat allegations of discriminatory lending to people in low income neighborhoods. According to the Federal Reserve board, the CRA encourages banks to "meet the credit needs of the communities in which they operate, including low- and moderate-income neighborhoods, consistent with safe and sound operations." In practice, it helped defeat a few cases of blatant redlining, and it blackmailed a few banks into making additional loans in bad neighborhoods. Thanks to the "safe and sound operations" clause, banks could not be pressured into making highly-risky loans.

The CRA did no great harm initially, but it was a ticking time bomb. It was a green light for politicians to stick their noses into the lending practices of private banks, and threaten penalties against those who didn't pander to Democrat constituents. It was ripe for abuse.

You can start paying attention now. This is where the trouble begins. In 1999, a New York Times story reported that the Clinton Administration pressured Fannie Mae to expand the number of mortgage loans given to low-income consumers. "Pressured" might be a bit of an overstatement. The CEO of Fannie Mae was, as usual, a Democrat party hack. In this case it was Franklin Raines, Clinton's former White House Budget Director. Raines was Clinton's man. If Clinton threw a stick, Raines was going to fetch it. If Clinton wanted Raines to make a pile of risky loans, it would be done.

The move was pure political pandering by Clinton, whose ego could always be reliably stroked by those who referred to him as our "first black President." It created undeserved loans for low-income constituents and funneled tens of millions to Clinton cronies like Raines.

Fannie Mae accomplished the expansion easily enough. All they had to do was tell lenders to go ahead and make high risk loans. Don't worry about it. We'll buy them from you. And that's what happened.

The Clinton Administration had snapped its fingers and changed the definition of creditworthiness. People with poor credit woke up one morning and found themselves eligible for enormous home loans. This is where the rock began rolling down the hill – when we started making six-figure loans to the financially challenged.

The housing market, like most free markets, tends to seek some sort of equilibrium. Based on the concepts of supply and demand, the number of houses built should approximate the number of consumers willing and able to purchase them. Suddenly, almost overnight, the number of people who could "afford" a house had increased dramatically.

The supply of eligible home buyers greatly exceeded the number of homes available. Home sales began to feel more like auctions, with the majority of sellers fielding multiple offers. The flood of new buyers sent home prices skyward. For the home construction industry it was Christmas all year long. Builders were selling newly-constructed homes as quickly as they could build them.

The buyers needed loans for these homes, and many of the new loans were of the subprime variety. There's a Wall Street saying that subprime is a euphemism for "junk." Subprime borrowers generally have poor credit. At some point in their history they have treated timely bill paying as optional. To make up for the additional risk in lending to such people, subprime loans have higher interest rates than the loans available to buyers with good credit.

When subprime loans are packaged into securities, the investments contain a higher level of risk, due to the shaky credit history of the people paying the underlying mortgages. But when the people do manage to make their mortgage payments, the investments pay off very nicely. For a few years, that's exactly what happened. Homeowners in financial trouble had no problem reselling their homes in the hot market. Most mortgages got paid, and the presumably risky investments paid off handsomely.

The demand for these investments grew rapidly. Investors around the world couldn't wait to tie themselves to the fates of lower/middle class Americans with spotty credit habits. The investments continued to pay off, and the demand for them continued to grow.

George W. Bush got into the act in 2002 with a goal of increasing minority home ownership by 5.5 million by 2010, and backing his plan with billions of federal dollars in cash and tax credits. Bush was a big believer in the concept of an ownership society. He believed that home ownership led to stable and prosperous communities, stable and prosperous families, and a stable and prosperous nation.

This overly sunny view of humanity is based in a logical fallacy. People who own their homes are statistically more likely to pay their bills on time, stay married, keep their children out of jail, hold steady jobs, regularly attend church, and send their children to college, but the home ownership does not cause these things. Responsible people who pay their bills are, through their actions, more likely to put themselves in a position to afford their own homes. The acquisition of a mortgage does not, in and of itself, make the holder more responsible.

Bush was the Jekyll and Hyde of this entire fiasco. Not long after pushing Fannie Mae to transform renters into owners, he recognized the potential danger of the move. In 2003, he proposed a new agency within the Treasury Department to supervise Fannie and Freddie, which the New York Times called "an acknowledgement by the administration that the oversight of Fannie Mae and Freddie Mac – is broken." Bush sent HUD Secretary Mel Martinez and Treasury Secretary John Snow to the Financial Services Committee meeting to push the proposal. Democrats objected to anything resembling real regulation. The proposal went nowhere.

The most notable product of the meeting was a statement from Barney Frank, then the ranking Democrat on the committee. Frank said, "These two entities — Fannie Mae and Freddie Mac — are not facing any kind of financial crisis. The more people exaggerate these problems, the more pressure there is on these companies, the less we will see in terms of affordable housing."

It's hard to see how someone could be more clueless or more wrong about an issue than Frank was on the issue of Fannie and Freddie. Fannie and Freddie were sick, and their disease almost collapsed our entire economy. In a sane world, Barney Frank would be a punch line. Towers would be erected to his monumental incompetence. What was Frank's punishment for such an epic miscalculation? He is now the Chairman of the House Financial Services Committee, where, from a pool of his own slobber, he continues to dispense his wisdom.

Here's something that should sound familiar to anyone following the Obama administration. In 2004, after regulators had found $9 billion in accounting errors at Fannie Mae, errors that had put tens of millions of dollars in the pockets of Franklin Raines and other Fannie execs, Raines was called to testify before a congressional committee. Faced with clear proof of gross, and perhaps criminal, mismanagement, Democrats lined up to excoriate the regulator!

Congressman Lacy Clay, a Democrat from Missouri, stated, "This hearing is about the political lynching of Franklin Raines." What had not been relevant previously now bears mentioning – Franklin Raines is black, and of course that changes everything. Racism is the only possible motivation for criticizing a black man. Barack Obama is hardly the first man to benefit from this bit of illogic, only the latest.

Raines later resigned from his position at Fannie Mae, but no steps were taken to regulate the runaway company. If anything, the post-Raines version of Fannie was even more reckless, backing increasingly riskier mortgages, including loans that did not require proof of income from borrowers.

Wall Street followed Fannie Mae's lead, and made some ridiculous moves. Firms like Bear Stearns, Goldman Sachs and Lehman Brothers gobbled up trillions in risky investments, leveraging their assets as much as 40 to 1. They pressured credit rating agencies to get suicidally-dangerous investments rated as safe. They played the Franklin Raines game better than Raines himself, and poured billions into the accounts of their top executives.

Back at the housing boom, nothing had changed. Mortgages could be had for a signature and a down payment of pocket lint. The homeowners who were unable to make their payments were allowed to refinance their homes, pull cash out of the deal, and use the cash to make their payments (or purchase shiny new cars). Investors consumed the new, even riskier, loans without pause.

It was all unsustainable. Even by the Clinton Administration's new standard, the market ran out of people who could "afford" to buy homes. Home prices decreased, setting off a chain reaction. People who couldn't afford their monthly payments were no longer allowed to refinance. They were forced into foreclosure. Fannie Mae, Freddie Mac and the banks were stuck with stacks of worthless paper. It had always been junk, but now that no one would buy it, it was also worthless.

When the dust cleared, numerous financial institutions failed or were sold. The government had to step in and take over Fannie Mae and Freddie Mac, which effectively nationalized them. At the time of the government takeover, Fannie and Freddie owned or guaranteed almost half of the United States' $12 trillion mortgage market.

Barack Obama is very selective when he assigns blame for the debacle. Perhaps it's nothing more than a well-worn reflex when he blames the Bush Administration. You get the feeling you could pull on the man's tie and a hidden speaker would recite, "It was broken when I got here."

There's nothing wrong with blaming Bush in this case, even if his biggest crime was an inability to understand that you can't turn deadbeats into upstanding citizens by giving them new houses.

Obama frequently blames the meltdown on a lack of regulation, but there is never a mention of the legislators who opposed regulation at every opportunity. There's no mention of Barney Frank, and there's certainly no mention of the Congressional Black Caucus, who seem to see racist motives beneath every rock.

If you're looking for the greatest portion of Obama's disdain, you need only look to his favorite boogieman – the private sector. He blames big banks and brokerage houses for the entire mess. He's fond of the phrase, "what started on Wall Street goes to Main Street," but that blame can only go so far, and it doesn't address the beginning of the problem. Blaming Wall Street for the financial meltdown is like showing up for the last five minutes of Star Wars and deciding that Skywalker kid should go to jail for murdering all those nice folks on the Death Star.

There's a lot more to the story than Wall Street. If you think Barack Obama doesn't know that, then you need to re-read Rule Number One.

In the meantime, the House has introduced the Community Reinvestment Modernization Act of 2009. The 61 sponsors, all Democrats, think the government should do more to encourage loans in low-income neighborhoods...

Chapter Sixteen

Looking Sheikh on Broadway

After eight years of delay, those allegedly responsible for the attacks of September 11th will finally face justice.

- Attorney General Eric Holder

You remember Khalid Sheikh Mohammed. We've all seen his pictures – the scruffy fat guy with the moustache, t-shirt, and enough chest hair to knit his own Persian rug. Picture Saddam Hussein fresh out of the bunker and you're on the right track.

You might also know him as the 9/11 mastermind, and the most prominent detainee at Guantanamo Bay. Since his 2007 confession to that crime and others, it seemed like only a matter of time until he was tried by a military tribunal and executed. That's what happens after a confession. There's a conviction and a sentence.

All of that changed on November 13, 2009, when Attorney General Eric Holder arrived with news straight from the Bright Ideas Department. Citizen-of-the-World Barack Obama had deemed it necessary that we show the assembled nations the power of the American justice system, so we were going to bring KSM into a civilian court, and try him in New York City, a few blocks from Ground Zero.

Why would this possibly be a bad idea? If you can't come up with 20 reasons, you're not really trying.

Some would call it the worst idea Obama has ever had. But wait. They would be wrong, because the idea wasn't Obama's at all. Eric Holder told the Senate he made the decision all by himself. He didn't even consult with Obama.

And I have a newly-repaired bridge in Minneapolis to sell you.

More likely, the conversation went something like this:

Obama: So here's what you're going to tell them. You made this decision by yourself. You're the Attorney General, dammit. You can make a high level decision.

Holder: Did we, uh, talk about the case before I made the decision?

Obama: Are you listening to what I'm telling you? This is not about me. Your decision. Your job. Comprende?

Holder: Um, yeah. Okay.

Obama: Okay. I'm going to be in Japan for a few days. So while I'm gone, that's when I want you to hold the press conference.

Holder: You... you aren't going to stand behind me during the announcement.

Obama: And have my face on the TV when people hear about this? I'll have to take a pass on that one.

Holder: But, Mr. President...

Obama: Let me be clear. When I gave you this job, I told you that some day you might have to take a bullet for me.

Holder: Mr. President, I was kind of hoping it would be an actual bullet. At least that way I wouldn't look like a complete idiot.

Obama: Ha ha. Well, Eric. Better you than me.

Holder: What?

Obama: Oh, did I say that out loud?

Think I'm exaggerating? The real life farce goes even further. When faced with questions about the possibility that KSM could be acquitted in a civilian court (you know, that whole innocent until proven guilty thing), the voices of the administration did not seem worried.

Vice President Biden seemed annoyed by the question, saying, "Look, there is no doubt that he would not be acquitted." The double-negative almost got me there.

White House spokesman Robert Gibbs clarified the matter, promising not only a conviction, but a prompt meeting with Allah. "Khalid Sheikh Mohammed is going to meet justice and he's going to meet his maker. He will be brought to justice and he's likely to be executed for the heinous crimes he committed."

When an NBC reporter suggested that some people might find it offensive that KSM was being afforded the rights of an American citizen, Obama himself said "I don't think it will be offensive at all when he's convicted and when the death penalty is applied to him."

It's like the old western where they can't decide whether to hang the horse thief or give him a fair trial. They finally decide to give him a fair trial, and then hang him.

Why were we doing this in the first place? Oh yeah, so the rest of the world would respect our justice system. Nice job, O.

Chapter Seventeen

What's It All About?

"It's not about me."

- Barack Obama

One of the highlights of Barack Obama's presidency occurred in a speech he delivered on February 4, 2010. It began as just another stop on the Democrat Death March to Socialized Medicine, but when he reached the part of the speech where it was time to insert one of his interchangeable sob stories of health care denied, he pulled out some new material.

There was a woman who worked on his campaign. She had, presumably through the machinations of George W. Bush, lacked health insurance. She had recently passed away after a long battle with breast cancer.

If you too have had the displeasure of hearing over 100 Obama health care speeches, this is the part of the speech where you run to the refrigerator. You've heard all of his sad stories, and some of them are a lot sadder than this one.

But his one is special. I'll let the president tell you the rest:

> *She had fought a tough battle for four years. All through the campaign she was fighting, but finally she succumbed. And she insisted she's gonna be buried in an Obama t-shirt.*

Can a megalomaniac receive a greater gift than one of his followers worshipping him from the grave? In that moment, basking in the glow of his own importance, Obama must have known how the pharaohs of Egypt felt as they watched the pyramids go up and their builders fall down.

Obama loves reminding us it's not about him. It's not about me – it's about health care. It's not about me – it's about the American people. It's not about me – it's about that poor woman who was buried in my t-shirt. Oh, I guess that's pretty much entirely about me. And isn't it cool? Do you think Roosevelt ever had one of his toadies buried in an FDR shirt? What about Nixon? Hah! Don't make me laugh.

During the 2008 campaign Obama would stand, surrounded by enough portraits of himself to make Chairman Mao jealous, and proclaim to his followers that the election was "not about me." It was easy to shrug that one off. Politicians say some absurd things during elections. He had already promised to lower the sea levels, so a comment like this barely registered.

A few months later, he reminded us, "This inauguration is not about me. It's about all of us." That was quite a day. It was very crowded up on that podium. Getting us all to repeat that oath at the same time took a lot of practice.

When Obama speaks about our country, the word "I" is pressed into unpaid overtime, while the word "we" seems to be off somewhere on a four-year holiday.

He reminded us in multiple town hall meetings, "I inherited a $1.3 trillion deficit." Whew. It's a good thing our country didn't inherit it. After so generously assuming the nation's debt, Obama has a big hill to climb. He would have to write at least another 40,000 autobiographies to drag himself out of that hole, and that's 30,000 more than he had planned. How can one man possibly write that many autobiographies? With the Obama system of logic it's possible. Most of them wouldn't be about him.

If Obama is to be believed, the issue of health care reform is not about him. To reinforce this, he traveled the country for the better part of a year, spouting the line at town halls in every job-starved town in America. Elyria, Ohio got the doublespeak version:

> *I want you to understand, this is not about me. This is not about me. This is about you. This is not about me; this is about you.*

You could almost set it to music.

Professional athletes have their own version of the line. As a free agent pitcher hops a plane for a fat offer in another town, he's almost guaranteed to tell you, "It's not about the money." The difference between sports fans and Obama voters is that the sports fans understand that the athlete is lying.

In a July 2009 closed-door meeting with a Democrat congressman, Obama received the bad news about his health plan. It was in trouble in the House. Without changes, there was a chance it might not pass.

He thought of all letters he had received – all the sad stories he had recited. What would happen to those people, and millions more, if he could not get this legislation passed? It was almost more than the president could bear.

He spoke to the congressman, and every ounce of caring in his heart poured out when he said, "You're going to destroy my presidency."

Chapter Eighteen

No Tax Cuts Yet

The recovery plan provides a tax cut – that's right,
a tax cut – for 95% of working families.

- Barack Obama

One of Obama's most effective lies, during the presidential campaign and beyond, was his promise of a tax cut to 95% of working families. Like most lies, its effectiveness relies upon the ignorance of the target. If you don't understand what a tax cut actually is you might be under the impression that you received one from Barack Obama in 2009 or 2010.

The campaign version of the plan involved a $500 tax credit to individual workers or $1000 to working married couples. The real life version that Obama signed in early 2009 lowered the amounts to $400/$800, and was known as the Making Work Pay tax credit. The name lends a not unintentional impression that work never paid until Barack Obama got here. Before his arrival, our only compensation was wampum.

It's worthwhile to investigate the difference between a tax cut and a tax credit. The Obama regime uses the two terms interchangeably, but they are not the same thing. They have different features, different effects, and they are put forward with differing intentions.

Tax cuts are not handouts. They are decreases in the percentage of tax paid on a worker's earnings. Here is why they work. People are encouraged to earn more – to produce more – with the understanding that they will get to keep more of each dollar they earn. The more a person earns, the more benefit he receives from the tax cut, and thanks to his increased efforts and productivity, the economy also benefits from the cut. That's why people who like growing economies like tax cuts.

A tax credit is different. It's a one-time handout. It does not encourage extra work or extra productivity. Since the Making Work Pay tax credit had a ceiling of $75,000, it actually managed to discourage productivity in some workers. People near this ceiling risked losing part or all of their tax credit if they chose to work harder and earn more.

To witness the difference between real tax cuts and one-time payments, we need only look to the George W. Bush administration. After the country experienced negative growth in two of the first three quarters of 2001, Bush signed a series of tax cuts that restored growth to the economy. From 2001 to 2007, the United States experienced 24 consecutive quarters of uninterrupted positive growth. That's worth repeating. For six straight years the economy grew in every quarter.

After the housing bust hit, the economy slowed. Bush was now hampered by a Democrat Congress, so another tax cut was out of the question. Congressional Democrats view tax cuts with the same enthusiasm as a vampire viewing a crucifix. Come to think of it, Congressional Democrats view a crucifix with the same enthusiasm as a vampire viewing a crucifix.

Bush eventually settled for a $300/$600 tax rebate, a one-time payout cut from the same mold as the Obama tax credit. To say it was no more than a Band-Aid on the ailing economy does ill service to Band-Aids. The economy continued to shed jobs as the country fell into its deepest recession in decades.

As an economic stimulus, a tax credit does manage to wrestle a few dollars from the government, distribute them to citizens, and inject those dollars back into the economy. A tax credit is better than nothing, but not much better. It's a one-time thing. It does not provide an ongoing benefit. More to the point, it is not a tax cut. Incorrectly referring to it as one does not make it one, even if you do it 1000 times, and even if the person doing it is Barack Obama.

The Making Work Pay tax credit was a ridiculous failure when compared to its stated goal of improving the economy. It's a roaring success if you think of it as a part of one of Obama's ongoing hobbies – the funneling of cash to those who have not earned it.

Making Work Pay was not simply a tax credit, it was an abominable construct known as a refundable tax credit. For those blissfully unfamiliar with the term, allow me to ruin your day.

A tax credit reduces the amount of tax you owe by the amount of the credit. You can lower your tax burden all the way down to zero if you have enough tax credits, but you can't go past zero.

A refundable tax credit does not concern itself with the annoying detail of whether or not you did any work, or earned any money, or actually paid any taxes. In 2009, a whopping 47% of our citizens paid nothing in federal income tax. Thanks to Obama's tax credit being refundable, these filers received $400 in money they didn't earn. Presumably each one of them will use their vast business acumen and the newfound $400 to open a factory that employs thousands. That'll solve unemployment.

So unless you like the sound of that, don't be fooled when Obama tells you you're getting a tax cut. Or, I should say, don't be fooled again.

And when a liberal tries to use the inevitable failure of Obama's plan as proof that tax cuts don't work, ask him "What tax cuts?"

Barack Obama:
By the Numbers

Number of legal papers authored by Obama as president of Harvard Law Review: **1, unsigned**

Nubmer of Senate bills written by Obama that went on to become laws: **2**

Percentage of roll call votes missed by Senator Obama during his time in the Senate: **24%**

Number of former lobbyists appointed by Obama to senior government postions: **40 and counting**

Number of days Obama served as President before being nominated for the Nobel Peace Prize:
12

First foreign leader Obama called after being inaugurated as President: **Mahmoud Abbas, PLO**

First television station interview granted by Obama after being inaugurated as President:
Al Arabiya, United Arab Emirates

Number of people required to replace Michelle Obama when she left her $316,962 Chicago hospital job: **zero, the job was downsized**

Number of rounds of golf played by Obama during his first 15 months in office: **32**

Number of rounds of golf played by George W. Bush during his 8-year presidency: **24**

Amount of money Barack Obama believes a doctor receives for amputating one of your limbs:
$30,000 - $50,000

Percentage of General Motors owned by the United States government after Obama's takeover:
60%

Number of troops requested by Afghanistan commander Stanley McChrystal, in order to secure victory in that war: **40,000**

Number of days Obama left his field commander twisting without a decision: **65**

Number of troops Obama chose to send to Afghanistan in a half-assed attempt to almost, but not quite, win the war: **30,000**

Price of a gallon of unleaded gasoline in January 2009: **$1.79**

Price of a gallon of unleaded gasoline in January 2010: **$2.73**